POLITICAL WRITINGS
FROM SOMEWHERE IN THE 99%

Merrill Ring

<u>Political Works</u>:
*The Ant and The Grasshopper: A
Response from the Left*
 Editor*: Pithy Progressive Polemics*
Editor*: Leftward Ho! (Corrected Edition)*

<u>Philosophy Books</u>:
Beginning With the Pre-Socratics

<u>Philosophy Papers</u>:
<u>www.independent.academia.edu/Merrill Ring</u>

Political Writings
From Somewhere in the 99%

Merrill Ring

PREFACE

In 2011 The American Institute for Progressive Democracy (TAIPD) decided to start an online journal of progressive political thought to be called *Progressive Democracy*. I was named editor.

I soon discovered that being editor required also writing. That wasn't a problem: I was perfectly willing to do so.

Over the years what I have ended up writing and publishing in *Progressive Democracy* has amounted to quite a few pieces. Since those writings are not tied in detail to political events of the day – though of course there are connections – they constitute a body of thought and work that is of some continuing interest in progressive political writing.

Hence my decision to publish them in book form.

Why do that now? Why stop in 2017? There is no deep reason, not even the fact that we are suffering through the Age of Trump. I had to stop somewhere and the number of essays was getting large.

When I call them essays, that is often quite a stretch. What the journal publishes – and even more relevantly what I frequently write - very rarely requires snuggling down for an extended read. In fact, we specialize in a type of 'essay' which is intended to be much shorter than found in most publications – they are called Pithy Polemics in the journal and quite a few of those are mine and republished here. In fact, if the Content page of the book is looked at carefully, it will be noticed that very many of the pieces don't even occupy a single page.

One series of these journal writings have been omitted from this collection. It has been independently published under the title *The Ant and The Grasshopper: A Response from the Left.* I also realized while preparing the material for this book that I had failed to complete the series entitled *Lessons in Liberty.* The members of that series which were published in *Progressive Democracy* are included here, but the project has not been finished, something that waits for another day.

As usual with writers, certain themes recur in different essays. More importantly, there is no big picture presented here. Isaiah Berlin made famous the saying 'The fox knows many things, but the hedgehog knows one big thing'. I am by nature a fox: what I have to say touches on many issues. but there is no attempt made to talk about everything and to pull the ideas into a single hedgehogish picture.

Nonetheless, what is published here are ideas firmly embedded in the progressive (liberal, social democratic) tradition. They, of course, are my versions of progressive ideas. However, I do think that others can find in these writings something of value. As a T-shirt my son wears says: *Think before it becomes illegal.*

CONTENTS

POLITICAL WRITINGS
FROM SOMEWHERE IN THE 99%

A Response To The Citizen's United Decision

I'm not a lawyer or legal scholar. I think my reaction to the Supreme Court's decision in the Citizens United case is fairly typical of ordinary intelligent folk. Three matters have struck me and others, all leading to a lessening of the respect for the Court.

1. The idea that some members of the Supreme Court have and are treating Corporations as Persons strikes intelligent outsiders as plainly ludicrous. A favorite cartoon of mine: one of the Latino geezers in the comic strip *La Cucaracha* declares that if corporations are persons he sure would like to date Victoria's Secret. We hear the Supremes talking of Corporations as Persons and we immediately think of what could happen to real persons – and that no corporation could possibly be subject to such things (being executed, having a hot date with, serving in the military, voting, being mayor or dog catcher, having a doctor's appointment, snoring....)

Now it may be that in certain respects corporations resemble persons – but so does my dog (and perhaps more so than a corporation.) But the Supremes have not held that, as a constitutional matter, dogs are persons. So why have they taken it as a matter of legal right that corporations should be treated in American law as persons? We outsiders think that no matter what the resemblance in this or that respect of a corporation to a person there is nothing that could reasonably lead an intelligent and unbiased person to declare them to be people with the full set of rights and responsibilities of an American person. The conclusion must be that the Supremes' education and intelligence have been overwhelmed by some form of prejudice.

2. The decision involves calling and treating Money as Speech: and as we are prohibited from restricting speech in this country so we are prohibited from restraining the use of money in speaking (politically). Now it is true, as we all know, that money talks. But that is precisely what runs counter to democratic ideals which have an assumption of basic political equality. If we allow Money to be Speech, as the Court does, we undermine our democratic ideals. For if you have

$1000 and I have $1, then you have the legal right to be 999 times more important in the political process than I am. It is not that you are superior to me in intelligence, education, concern, knowledge, wisdom and therefore you should be listened to more than me. It is just that you have a lot more money than me – and that can be freely used to push your political views without regard to the important distinctions between people that make one person's views better than another's.

Money is not Speech – it is a medium of exchange that enables persons to do or purchase things they desire. When what is done or purchased is a political matter, that is a point of concern for those addicted to democracy, a legitimate reason for legal restraints on the use of money to affect political decisions. It is shocking to ordinary people that persons as intelligent and as educated as the Justices of the Supreme Court declare that money should freely talk and talk extremely loudly in our democracy, in effect rendering it formally a plutocracy.

3. If it is objected that the *Citizen's United* decision is merely the latest in a line of decisions treating Corporations as Persons and treating Money as Speech and that hence precedent means that the court is correct in reaching the conclusion that it did in the recent case, we outsiders can only think that that is a mad view of the role of precedent in normal human life and in legal decisions (in so far as we understand the legal status of precedent.) Surely those who made the original decision were people and so subject to error. To argue that the Court must have come to the conclusion that it did in *Citizen's* because it has been written in stone that Corporations are Persons and that Money is Speech strikes us as madness. The lemming who leaps because all those who preceded him/her have done so has should not be the principle of human life and of legal decisions. Try this principle: Think! Emerson said that consistency was the virtue of small minds: to encourage the above kind of respect to precedent reveals nothing but a small (or lemming) mind. The poem goes 'Oh what a tangled web we weave when first we practice to deceive.' The same goes when we blindly follow the mistakes others have made in pursuit of nothing other than consistency.

How Corporations Became People In The Eyes Of The Supreme Court

Many Americans have been deeply upset by the realization that our Supreme Court holds that corporations are persons. How could such an absurd proposition have become part of the American legal tradition? Here is the story.

To the best of my knowledge what I say here is correct, at least on the major points. Should I be mistaken I would be very pleased to learn the truth.

I shall summarize Thom Hartmann's account in his book *Unequal Protection* (I urge people to read the full account in Chapter 1 of that book.) Hartmann was not the first to have noticed many of the relevant points but he has the best overall non-academic presentation. On crucial points about the history as Hartmann presents it, I have not found any major criticisms (there are several points of unclarity in his account.)

This story is both historically interesting and quite important as it should play some role in our attempt to overturn Citizen's United. To that end, I have sprinkled some pieces of my own commentary in the narrative.

Pre-14thAmendment

A distinction between *natural* and *artificial* persons – the latter being (at least chiefly) corporations – was originally worked out in English common law (the history of that development I don't know). The point of the distinction was to treat corporations as a kind of person in order to justify various matters pertaining to their legal status: as artificial persons they could own property, sign contracts, be taxed, sue and be sued in courts. The distinction between the two kinds of person was discussed in the authoritative commentary on the common law by

William Blackstone published in the 18th century, a work known to the writers of the constitution and still cited by the Supreme Court in decisions. As the English common law became the basis of American law, we inherited that distinction.

If the notion of corporate personhood is abolished via constitutional amendment, the legal system will still have to have a means of recognizing the above features of the legal status of corporations (what is to be excluded by any amendment are the rights to *political speech* that Citizens United gave them.) However, it is a huge intellectual and consequently political error to base those rights on the common law claim that corporations are <u>any</u> kind of person as the common law did and does. Post-amendment they should not be thought of as artificial persons but as quite some other kind of institutional entity.

14th Amendment

The 14th amendment (proposed by Congress in 1866, ratified by the states in 1868) provided equal protection of the law for all persons. The intent of this post-Civil War amendment was to wipe out legal distinctions between blacks and whites. However, the language of the amendment says "persons" not "natural persons" which, in light of the existing legal distinction between natural and artificial persons, it should have said to secure the intent of the amendment.

Not long after the amendment was accepted two Congressmen instrumental in writing the amendment, Senator Roscoe Conkling and Representative John Bingham, went on to become lawyers for the railroads - the major corporations in those days. Conkling bragged in a court case that it was they who had seen to it that the phrase "natural person" was not used in the 14th but only "person".

That language opened the door for corporations to argue that, since they were already a kind of person by common law, they were now entitled to equality with all other persons.

The 14th was passed hurriedly, with supporters admitting that they hadn't taken time to think through all the details. There was thus no Congressional discussion of whether the amendment concerned what had been known as 'artificial persons', i.e. corporations, no debate on whether the 14th was to give corporations equal protection under the law with living breathing American citizens. That legislative failure left it up to the law as to whether corporations were to be covered by the 14th.

1886: Southern Pacific Railroad v Santa Clara County

This was the crucial case that, according to legal scholars, established that, in light of the 14th amendment, corporations were persons and entitled to equal protection under the law with all other persons.

The case was a tax dispute that worked its way up to the Supreme Court. Southern Pacific's lawyers argued that Santa Clara County had wrongly taxed some railroad property. Their case had six different lines of argument. One of those arguments, carried on at some length, made appeal to the 14th amendment and claimed that the constitution had now made the railroad a person with consequences for the tax dispute.

The Court ruled for the railroad – but it did so on the narrow ground that the assessment of the property was conducted by the wrong agency. The decision said among much else: "These questions [regarding the 14th] belong to a class which this court should not decide unless their determination is essential to the disposal of the case…. Whether the present cases require a decision of them [the constitutional issues] depends upon the soundness of another proposition, upon which the court… in view of its conclusions upon other issues, did not deem it necessary to pass…. If these positions are tenable, there will be no occasion to consider the grave questions of constitutional law … as the judgment can be sustained upon this ground, it is not necessary to consider any other questions raised by the pleading." That is, the court did not consider the constitutional issue raised by the railroad, and objected to by the defense, because it could find sufficient ground to come to a decision quite independently of the 14th amendment to the constitution.

Thus, the Court in the case that is thought to have established that corporations are persons did not consider the issue at all. Nonetheless it turns out that the entire American legal tradition thinks that the issue was discussed by the court in that case and decided in favor of corporate personhood.

The serious question comes up: how did that happen?

The Headnote

Hartmann considers some theories as to how it has come about that lawyers and judges believe that the 1886 case produced a decision that corporations were equally persons along with you and me. His own theory is this – and he argues it well.

The relevant decision (like all others) was published by the court reporter, a J.C. Bancroft Davis. At that time the court reporter was not a stenographer as he/she is today. Bancroft Davis was a significant political figure – he actually was paid more in his job than were any of the justices. At one time, 20 years previously he had been on the board of directors of a railroad.

When he published the decision, he included in the publication what are called 'headnotes' – commentary on the case by someone such as himself who had no part in the decision. Headnotes thus have no legal standing. In his headnote to this case Bancroft Davis wrote "One of the points made and discussed at length in the brief of counsel for defendants in error was that 'Corporations are persons within the meaning of the Fourteenth Amendment to the Constitution of the United States.' Before argument Mr. Chief Justice Waite said: 'The court does not wish to hear argument on the question whether the provision in the Fourteenth Amendment … which forbids a State to deny to any person within its jurisdiction the equal protection of the laws, applies to these corporations. We are all of the opinion that it does."

Bancroft Davis' claim in the headnote that Chief Justice Waite said that his fellow justices agreed that corporations are persons is the source of the legal belief that the case settled that they are. By the time the decision was published (about 1½ years later) Waite was virtually dead and so he had no ability to see it. It is Hartmann's thesis that Bancroft Davis took it upon himself to include the comment in the headnote. The legal tradition has come to believe that the abstract (which is what a headnote amounts to) by Bancroft Davis of what the justices believed is what the decision said.

But the court explicitly denied that the constitutional issue had a bearing on their decision.

Following the Southern Pacific case, corporations leaped to make use of the idea that the court had ruled that constitutionally they were full-fledged legal persons. Hartmann notes that the 14th was not applied to women and to blacks until the 20th century – no matter what its language and intent – but corporations immediately began arguing on its basis over and over in cases affecting them. It was a corporate coup.

Harry Belafonte sang 'House built on a weak foundation will not stand.' The idea of corporate personhood as constitutionally guaranteed has been built on a phantom foundation – but it stands because it is enshrined in the American legal tradition, serving as precedent in so many Supreme Court rulings.

Inheritance Taxes: The Conservative Contradiction

The Progressive/Liberal and the Conservative have very different views as to 'death duties' – the Conservative should in principle demand that a received estate should be taxed away, the Progressive is much more supportive of family values.

Sometimes it is called an estate tax, sometimes an inheritance tax ('death duty' is the misleading and informal name.) It should make a difference which of those names is attached to the tax, though in practice (around the world so far as I can see) one or the other name is used without any thought given to the matter.

Now while market liberals (neo-liberals) think there should be no taxes or perhaps some very small taxation to support no more than 'the night-watchman state', that particular form of taxation with the two names is high on their list of condemned forms of taxation. Yet the principles by which they condemn it are contradictory.

First, as to the names. To call something an 'estate tax' should be to conceive of it as a tax levied on a person's resources when he or she dies and before the resources are passed on to a later generation. On the other hand, an inheritance tax would be a tax to be paid by the inheritor on the resources they have acquired by inheriting them. The question of the appropriate name is relevant to the issue of what the <u>point</u> of the tax is.

Now the conservative will say that the person whose estate it is has the right to dispose of it as they see fit. Supposing that the resources - money, land, whatever - have been legitimately acquired (at least by normal social understanding of what is legitimate), then they are the person's property, having been acquired by the person's own effort, by the sweat of their brow, through their work. Then, the conservatives say, that person has the right to dispose of what is theirs as they wish and no one else, certainly not the state, has the right to interfere.

The problem in the conservative view, what they overlook in insisting upon the freedom to dispose of one's resources, is not with the disposal but with their receipt by the heir. Have the resources been acquired by the inheritor by their own effort, by the sweat of their brow, by their work? Overwhelmingly the answer is No – in the standard case such resources are received because the inheritors are the off-spring or other relatives of those who give. It is not a matter of work and receiving the fruits of one's labor – which is the conservative view of what rightly belongs to us individually. It is a matter of transmission to a family member of resources that he/she has not earned themselves from the sweat of their brow. Hence on the very principle that conservatives use to justify freedom to *give* the resources, the recipient does not warrant, is not justified in, *having them*.

A thoughtful and principled economic conservative would <u>demand</u> that there be a very large, if not complete tax on resources inherited. Each individual must possess resources only if they have engaged in work and earned the rewards of that effort. The older generation, thus, has the right to dispose of their property as they see fit – the younger generation, however, has no right to have it. Tax it away – support the night-watchman state from those resources.

But of course existing economic conservatives are not thoughtful and principled in this matter. They stand with the wealthy. They ignore their principles when it comes to matters of inheritance.

What should a progressive say about the tax? First, we should call it and think of it as a tax levied not on a person's estate at death but on the inheritor. However, since we do not have the same principles regarding work and what should rightfully belong to one, we do not have to think that a good inheritance tax would remove all or nearly all of what is inherited, leaving the younger generation to stand only upon their own two feet. We progressives are willing to give people a hand, an opportunity, as witnessed by progressive redistribution schemes. And families, not just individuals, are a part of our view of human life. Transferring some resources from one generation to the next is a humanly important way of giving people a hand while maintaining family structures.

But there are others in our society who deserve a better standard of living than has come to them by the contingencies of life. Consequently, an inheritance tax makes sense as a matter of redistribution. The problem for the progressive is to find the right level of inheritance taxation: one that does not maintain undesirable and undeserved inequality, but recognizes that it is right to help our children, as well as strangers, to achieve a decent life.

Note: in case you don't think that inherited money plays an important role in giving people a head-start in economic life in this country, consult the recent report *Born on Third Base: What the Forbes 400 Really Says about Wealth & Opportunity in America* (from the non-profit <u>United for a Fair</u> <u>Economy</u> – see <u>www.faireconomy.org</u>) It takes $1.1 billion to make the top 400 this year. Twenty percent of those on the list simply inherited enough to make the list. Another twenty percent inherited not quite enough to make it and had to supplement the "sizeable asset" they inherited by some other means. Keeping it in the family, seventeen percent of the 400 had another family member on the list. Those are major signs of the dynastic wealth in this country.

Lessons in Liberty (Part 1)

We Americans boast of our freedom – but we rarely stop to think about what freedom is. Philosophers and political theorists distinguish two types of liberty: if we are to think about our freedom we must take that distinction into account.

At least in belief though not in practice, the United States has from the beginning treated freedom as its central value. From Patrick Henry's 'Give me liberty or give me death' to New Hampshire's state motto 'Live free or die' we have extolled freedom as what we are all about.

Of course, there has equally long been a sub-current, at least one other value that gets mentioned when we pause briefly to think about it. That comes out in the Pledge of Allegiance: 'With liberty and justice for all.' Justice, fairness – that too is something we as a country are supposed to value, even if it does not often come at the top of our list.

What I want to talk about here (and in this series of essays) is the very concept of freedom. I am not so much interested in how deeply freedom has shaped our psyches and our public pronouncements. I am interested in discussions about the nature of freedom. That is a philosophical topic: one about the concept and not the practice of freedom.

An examination of the nature of freedom is especially appropriate in today's political world: there is a recent strain of political thought that perpetually cries 'Freedom'. I have in mind of course the Tea Party phenomenon – not the one in 1773 but the views that arose during the Obama presidency and did so in response to progressive support of, especially, the bank bailout and the Affordable Care Act.

For the new tea party people and for their billionaire backers, what freedom is is obvious: keeping the government from having any restraints on people's and corporations' (economic) behavior. Is that how we should think of freedom? Is that what it is all about? There is a long tradition that says yes – and an equally long tradition that says no. It is that dispute that I want to examine in these essays on freedom.

Ask any political philosopher about freedom and they almost surely will start (as philosophers typically do) by making a distinction. There is, they will say, on the one hand negative freedom and on the other positive freedom. Moreover, those two types of liberty are usually thought to be in conflict.

What is negative freedom? It is the sort of thing free marketers, conservatives, corporations, and today's tea partyers have in mind. It is freedom *from* – freedom from others having a right to interfere with one's own behavior. If I want to sell you bananas, a pure system of negative freedom would say that I have the right to do so without any interference from others, especially no interference from government regulations.

Of course, the proponents of negative freedom, at least the sensible ones, see that in a civilized society there must be some restrictions on my liberties to act as I please. My desire to hit you over the head with a baseball bat or to release sarin gas as I please must be interfered with, prevented if possible, be subject to penalty and punishment if I go ahead and act freely. Possibly only the so-called 'Sovereign Citizen' movement thinks otherwise.

Practically speaking, the debate over negative liberty concerns just where to draw the line between what a person should be free to do and what constitutes an infringement on that freedom. Parents are conceded the right to prohibit their children from engaging in certain kinds of behavior. But where does that stop? Should a 15 year old girl be free to have an abortion without notification of her parents? Should a high school newspaper be free to publish what its editors want or does the school have the right to step in and interfere with that freedom?

In the long standing debate between negative and positive liberty, there is no disagreement (perhaps other than by complete totalitarians) that a society that values freedom must encourage as much negative liberty as is consistent with an equal amount of freedom for everyone.

But the champions of positive liberty insist that there are important considerations built into the very concept of freedom that play a big role in deciding where to draw the line between what one is free to do and what must be interfered with for the general good, for the greatest amount of freedom.

What is positive liberty? Consider this: I am free to drive my car to work but the exercise of that freedom requires that I have a car. Positive liberty has to do with the conditions under which one can exercise the freedoms one has. Sometimes people do not have the ability to do what they have the right to do, what they are negatively free to do.

Perhaps the most powerful expression of the importance of what is called positive liberty is from an account of the situation of former slaves after the Emancipation Proclamation: "In 1865 emancipation from chattel slavery permitted black Americans one kind of freedom. No one would deny that this freedom [note that this is negative liberty] was a significant and meaningful one.... Yet this freedom was incomplete.... Land redistribution was aborted and the blacks were forced to begin their lives as free men and women without money, without tools, without work animals, without assets of any kind....The economic institutions established in the post-emancipation era effectively operated to keep the black population a landless agricultural labor force, operating tenant farms with a backward and unprogressive technology." [From R.L. Ransom and R. Sutch, *One Kind of Freedom: The Economic Consequences of Emancipation*, 1977]

The freed slaves had negative freedom, no one was any longer in a legal position to interfere with what they could do – but they were totally lacking in the wherewithal to do anything with that freedom: and so we say that they were (still) not free to live their lives as they would wish, that, despite the legal situation, they were not free to do what they (might have) wanted to do.

It is not only economic conditions that limit people's ability to exploit their freedom. If you make a promise or have a sick child, you are no longer free to do what you otherwise would have done, not because anyone is coercing you or because of your economic situation but because of moral relationships. If you are a runner on first base in a baseball game, you are free (to try) to steal second, but your broken toe may stand in the way of your trying: physical constraints may also limit your ability to exercise your (negative) freedom.

While every American, given our ideological commitment to freedom, ought to know the terms 'negative' and 'positive' freedom and know what the distinction is, we should also know that philosophically to draw the distinction as being between two kinds of freedom is not quite right. It is probably better just to talk of freedom and to recognize that various kinds of condition – economic, moral, physical – often interfere with our ability to exercise our freedoms, make us less free.

It seems to liberal philosophers that it is important both to ensure that people have as much freedom as possible consistent with others having the same freedoms and also have the means of exercising as much of that freedom as can be arranged. But those issues are the subject of the next essay in this series.

Lessons in Liberty (Part 2)

As human beings, as natural and social creatures, complete freedom to pursue our own desires is impossible and undesirable anyway. Given that freedom functions as the norm, what limits on freedom are justifiable?

While we Americans – especially those on the right - loudly, proudly and often - declare our dedication to freedom, we aren't much given in our public conversations to talking about what it is we are so dedicated to. The aim in this series of essays is to raise the philosophical question 'What is freedom?' and then to talk about some of the chief issues connected to freedom, especially as it pertains to our political lives.

Political philosophers and other theorists begin to address that question with a distinction between negative and positive liberty and treat those two conceptions as opposed.

Negative freedom is freedom from another's power over oneself and so from laws, rules and regulations devised by authorities to regulate our behavior. To be fully free in this way is for an individual to be completely self-determining. If you threaten to shoot me if I walk down your street, I am not free to walk down your street no matter what I want to do. What I can do is not determined by myself. If there is a law - and of course to be a law is to have a punishment attached for violation of the law - that I may not use a certain street, I am equally not free to pursue my own desires. In such cases, a person has not their full allotment of (negative) freedom.

Positive freedom is usually characterized as freedom to: there may be no kind of law or rule or blind power preventing someone from going to the movies tonight, but that person would not have the positive freedom to do so if they have no money to buy a ticket or if there is no movie theater in town.

In these essays I will not be treating those matters as two kinds of freedom standing in opposition to each other. There is some reason to draw the distinction that way. However, it is best, and I am not being idiosyncratic in this, to think of positive freedom as having the means of exercising one's freedom, having the wherewithal to make use of the opportunities created by (negative) freedom.

In American political discourse, these issues about freedom separate the various groups. What might be called left-wing libertarians, an increasingly small group, the remnants of the pure libertarian position, are defenders of (what is called) negative freedom, urging the most extensive amount of freedom from the power of others over the individual, freedom from laws and rules, and disliking any hint of positive freedom, any attempt to provide people with what is needed to make use of all that freedom. The right-wing libertarians, who are the majority part of the old libertarian position today, have joined the conservatives in being advocates of (negative) freedom in the economic sphere only. For the contemporary conservative, adherence to (negative) freedom in the economic sphere is married to a willingness to restrict freedom in the non-economic, the broadly social, areas of life (no freedom to marry someone of the same sex, denial of the freedom to have abortions, etc.) – right-wing libertarians silently go along with those attempts as economic life is taken to be central and crucial to human freedom.

The left, the liberals and social democrats, on the other hand, insist that we as a nation must not only aim at as much freedom as possible, especially in people's non-economic lives, but also that we must act to enable people to make full use of their freedom. Enabling people to exercise their freedom typically involves the imposition of taxes and regulations on other people, thereby limiting their freedom to act as they and they alone see fit economically.

Those differences between the left and the right will have to be considered again later. However, the first task in talking about the nature of freedom is thinking about what is traditionally called negative freedom.

No one believes that we are totally free. The world around us limits our options: for example. we human beings cannot survive, even if we would want to, without water. We are social animals and finding our natural place to be in a society of fellow humans, we are confronted from day one with rules, laws, customs and such. We may get rid of some of them – we grow up and the rules set up by our parents are left behind; bad laws are often eliminated - but what doesn't vanish is the existence of sets of laws and regulations by which a society is organized.

And that is a good thing: my freedom to do as I please is rightly limited. I am not free to hit you over the head without consequences and you are not free in the same way. Some laws are there to protect us from harms caused by others – the law against assault is a limitation of freedom, one that we (almost) all welcome.

Given that no thoughtful person wants laws and rules to vanish completely so that everyone has freedom without any (social) limits, the questions are: how extensive freedom should we have and what kinds of reasons may be used to justify limiting it. Look at a non-political case: soccer rules require players to have their jerseys tucked into their shorts. Is that limitation on a player's freedom desirable? What kind of justification can be given for it? Those same questions arise in politically relevant cases – it will turn out that the debate between the left and the right on the matter of freedom is a debate over, especially, what kinds of justification are to be offered for limiting freedom, e.g. can any form and degree of income redistribution (taking money from the better off to assist the worse off) be justified as a limitation on liberty?

The assumption of our political thought and talk is that freedom is the norm and that what must be justified (or, in the case of limits set by physical nature, simply accepted) are restrictions on an individual's liberty. We are not living in a totalitarian world in which unfreedom is the norm and what must be defended is giving people liberties.

Moreover, what is assumed in this country is that people should share equally in freedom – that you have an entitlement to hit me over the head with a baseball bat while I'm not free to do that to you is assumed to be unfair. But of course we sometimes act to justify unequal treatment: you can be locked up and deprived of your freedom and I can't be but that is because you have committed a crime and I haven't. Or you can be required to have your factory stop polluting the air and I not have any such requirement imposed on me - but that is because you own a factory and I don't. Again, what is required in such cases is that unequal treatment in depriving people of specific freedoms must be justified.

It is obvious that in practice the kinds of case to which these principles of freedom are applied are enormous. As this is intended to be an essay in philosophy, the aim here is not to examine freedom on a case by case basis. Rather what needs to be discussed next are the kinds of justification that we, in a political context, might use to limit freedom.

Lessons in Liberty (Part 3)

Is it morally legitimate to restrict someone's freedom? Of course, it is. Contrary to Rand Paul, even freedom to do with one's property what one wants can be rightly restricted as it was by the Civil Rights Act of 1964.

No matter how deeply committed to freedom Americans are, they talk more about it than think of what it is. These essays on freedom are intended to address philosophical issues about the nature of freedom.

The starting place in the project must be the distinction between negative and positive freedom. If someone ties you up or a government requires you to pay taxes you are not free to act, even if you are pleased at being tied up or happy to be paying taxes. There are constraints on your actions that limit your freedom. Freedom from constraints is what is meant by 'negative freedom'. On the other hand, positive freedom is having the ability to do what you otherwise are free to do: even if you are not in jail you might not have the <u>resources </u>to do what the absence of constraints leaves you free to do, for example buy your daughter a new dress or see a doctor about your persistent cough.

Although we should all know that terminology, I shall not be treating negative and positive freedom as two different kinds of freedom. There is some reason for doing that but it is best to treat positive freedom as a a matter of having the means to pursue activities that you are free to do – and so the absence of 'positive freedom' is special kind of limit on the exercise of freedom conceived of as doing what I please without interference. Just as one cannot, say, go on a vacation to New Jersey if one is in jail, you may not be able to go because you don't have the money. There are obviously important differences between those two kinds of restriction on freedom but there are also very important similarities.

It is necessary to begin a further discussion by concentrating on negative freedom. I pointed out in the first of these essays that no one is free to do whatever they might choose to do. Superman can fly to the top of a building – the rest of us cannot, even if we should like to do so. The world puts all manner of constraints upon we humans. There are also constraints of time and place: we 21st century Americans cannot have the same view of the world as a contemporary New Guinea tribesman or see the world as our grand-mother did. In our adult lives we were shaped by the public world into which we were born and cannot be something other than that: we whose first language is English must accept that as a fact about ourselves that cannot be otherwise.

Everyone in their right mind recognizes that there are certain desirable limits on imposed upon an individual's freedom. That you have no right to shoot me should you choose to do so is very valuable to me (and others) and is the result of imposing a restriction on your freedom. Of course, I must accept that I too have my freedom restricted when I am denied the right to shoot you even if that is what I want to do. What that means is that we value *equality* in restraints upon people's freedom. We do not live in a social world in which members of one class of people can, say, shoot others of a different class at their pleasure with legal justification, whereas shoot-able people do not have the freedom to respond in kind.

This equality in restrictions upon a person's freedom does not mean reciprocity. If your factory pollutes my drinking water and I don't have a factory, I can't be restrained from polluting your drinking water by my factory. So any regulation or law that produces a restraint upon your ability to do as you please with your factory's waste cannot apply to me. But that does not mean that we are not being treated as equals simply because I don't have a constraint on my freedom that you do. The best that be said is that if I were to have a factory I would be subject to the same law restraining my freedom. That is what equality means in this kind of case.

The question about negative freedom is not 'Should there be any legal constraints on our freedom to act?' – the right wing story about the completely free man is a giant myth – but 'What constraints should there be?'

In turning to that issue, the first and very important point must be to notice that freedom is our norm – that what must be done is to justify restrictions on people's freedom. Our is not a totalitarian society in which people (or at least most of them) are not normally free and what must be defended is a relaxation of restrictions, allowing people to do as they please. Part of the American story is that we are a freedom loving people and what that means is that we expect constraints on people's freedom to act will have to be justified. The burden of proof is on those who would limit (negative) freedom.

In pursuing this matter I will not be considering every kind of case, every circumstance in which we deal with issues of constraints on freedom. Standard moral obligations are restrictions on our freedom – marriages normally are ways of restricting what we are free to do – families have rules as do schools – and so on. Rather I am interested here (as befits this journal of political opinion) on restrictions roughly falling within the public sphere: laws and such passed by government.

A Complete Misconception of Freedom

Senator Rand Paul, the most widely known face of libertarianism, in his Senate campaign in 2010 said that the Civil Rights Act of 1964 had to go because of its provisions eliminating discrimination in the marketplace: in preventing restaurant owners (say) from refusing to serve people on the basis of their race ('You may not sit at my lunch-counter'), it was a violation of the freedom of those property owners to do with their property as they see fit. He added (crocodile tears?) that allowing discrimination is "the hard part of believing in freedom".

Does "believing in freedom" require that there can be no situation in which some other value requires limiting freedom? Of course not – as I've said above, people speaking thoughtlessly, as Paul does, blithely ignore the kinds of case where he would surely agree that freedom is rightly restricted: I am not free to help myself to your wallet. One can and, if one is rational – and libertarians place all their bets on being rational – <u>must</u> agree that no matter how important freedom is, it is not the only valuable thing and that in order to protect, possibly even further other freedoms, certain kinds of freedom must be legally restrained.

That is exactly what the Civil Rights Act does: to ensure your freedom (if you are an ethnic minority or someone else likely to be subject to discrimination) it prohibits those engaged in the marketplace, in business activity, from certain kinds of discrimination. While judging the quantity of freedom is messy, it is highly likely that there is a net gain in freedom achieved by prohibiting the forms of discrimination covered by the Civil Rights Act.

Could not Senator Paul, claiming to believe in freedom, have made that calculation, seen that consequence of the Act? Of course he could have. Why didn't he? Is it really true, as he implies, that discrimination is abominable – but that it is less important than the freedom to do with one's property what one wills, even if that property is employed in market activity? That is no doubt that is exactly what he believes.

But then the issue is not whether one "believes in freedom" – defenders of the Civil Rights Act are such believers and do not cease believing in freedom simply because they take it that discrimination is a restraint on the freedom of those wishing to sit at the lunch-counter. And such defenders believe that it is a significant diminution of some people's freedom that the owner's freedom must be restricted.

Contrary to Senator Paul, the issue is whether property rights are more important in our value system than the freedom of others to enjoy access to what is put on the market. The issue is not whether freedom trumps everything, but whether the freedom associated with property rights trumps the freedom of others to be full participants in economic activities. The libertarian (Rand Paul) says yes – the Civil Rights Act (rightly) says no. So it is not freedom or no freedom, as Paul claims it to be, but rather weighing different freedoms and finding that one has a stronger moral claim than another.

Lessons in Liberty (Part 4)

Reasons must be given for restraining the exercise of our freedom. Case: what justifies the requirement that people be vaccinated against infectious diseases?

Gliding over many important details, the upshot of the previous essays in this sequence is that this country's commitment to freedom (what is typically called 'negative freedom') requires that the burden of proof rests upon those who would restrict freedom in specific ways and cases. It is not that we are committed to freedom in such a way that no restrictions on it can be justified, as the libertarians (see Senator Rand Paul) attempt to hold. There are many justified restrictions, which can be recognized without in the slightest surrendering a commitment to freedom as a central value.

The serious question concerns the considerations that enable us to properly defend restrictions on people's freedom to do as they wish.

I won't be trying to work out a complete list (if that is possible) of possible lines of justification for restricting freedom. Rather what I shall be doing is to consider some of the prominent reasons for holding that in certain kinds of case, someone's freedom must be restrained in this or that way and to this or that degree. For instance, I mentioned previously that to accept freedom in the market place does not mean that we can accept discrimination against some minority at the lunch counter. If you are to engage in a business, in a market activity, your freedom to discriminate against possible customers (or employees) can rightly be denied since that exercise of your freedom amounts

to an unjustified interference with the freedom of those discriminated against. It does not follow, however, that you must serve a drunk or hire a drunken employee.

As I write this a case of a similar sort is roiling American political discourse. It is the issue of vaccinations, in this case against measles. Some people are refusing to have their children vaccinated against measles and are thus contributing to the spread of a serious infectious disease.

Now of course it is possible to think that what ought to be done, given our commitment to an individual's liberty (and in this case that of a parent's freedom to see that their children are properly treated), is to convince each of the disbelieving parents that they are mistaken about the efficacy of the vaccination and the absence of serious harm that the children might run if vaccinated. Or, differently, to convince them by argument that they are also causing a serious problem for others by this exercise of their freedom.

But those solutions would all take substantial time to accomplish and, moreover, are not even as efficacious as the vaccinations would be, given the ability of some people to resist rational persuasion. So the strategy is to require vaccinations of all the relevant children: pass a law that restricts the freedom of the parents by making them have their children vaccinated, subject to penalties for non-compliance.

Now can that solution be accepted, not just in panic but rationally, upon reflection, by we who are committed to freedom? Surely it can. Crudely put, the case correctly concludes that the public welfare, the public good, is such that it outweighs, in the relevant circumstances the parents' freedom to do what they think best for their children.

Lessons in Liberty: The Common Good (Part 5)

Freedom is something we care for deeply – but it is not the only thing of value to us. People's freedom can be restrained without denying that liberty is a major aim of our political lives. But such restraints must be justified. What justifications are used, can be used, in political life, to properly restrain people from doing what they want?

In the previous essay I examined one particular case in some detail: the justification for requiring people to have vaccinations, whether for smallpox or measles. The justification for doing so is that it is for the common good, that not being vaccinated places other people at risk and to prevent harm it is necessary to require that people be vaccinated.

What about that notion of 'the common good' appealed to in defending the restriction on people's liberty?

There are other terms roughly equivalent to 'the common good': 'the general welfare' (as that occurs in the Preamble to the U.S. Constitution) and 'the public interest' are approximate variants. Here, however, I shall prefer the phrase 'the common good'.

Appealing to the common good certainly does occur in American political discourse. We talk of some course of action or policy which typically requires some group of people to do something that they may not of their own will wish to do or it forbids some from doing something they may well want to do: and we justify that by saying that it is for the common good. A requirement that people do such and such in order to achieve the common good constrains people from pursuing their private good.

Although the common good is a notion alive in American political talk and thought (I notice also that Pope Francis appealed to it in his comments before Congress), it is not without problems.

The libertarians, inheriting the view from Ayn Rand, hold that there is no such thing as the common good. Their view is justified by saying that since only individuals exist, there is no common good. They of course mean by "individuals" individual human beings.

The premise of libertarian argument is quite wrong. There are also organizations: The United Nations came into being, into existence, in 1945 and is not even composed of individual people. Contrary to the Supreme Court, General Electric (etc.) is an organization and not a person, not an individual. One wishes the Klu Klux Klan no longer existed but sadly it does.

In trying to deny that society or the state or the public exists, libertarians defend a form of political atomism parading as metaphysical atomism.

Not only is the premise false, but the conclusion, that therefore there is no common good, doesn't follow. More of that in a minute.

However, rejecting the libertarian view does not solve all the problems with the notion of the common good. For it can still be asked, in a philosophical tone of voice, 'What kind of thing is the common good?' Here there are two conflicting answers.

The modern liberal tradition shares with its libertarian cousins the atomistic idea that only individuals exist, but holds that nonetheless sense can be made of the concept of the common good. For liberal thought, the common good for a political order can be determined by adding up the preferences of its individual citizens where everyone's preference counts equally.

(Actually Ayn Rand, unlike her libertarian off-spring, more or less accepted that possibility. "...there is no such thing as 'the public interest' (other than the sum of the individual interests of its individual citizens.)" She starts by denying that there is such a thing as the common good, but then ends by granting what the liberal tradition holds to be the way of making sense of the notion.)

Modern progressives (often called communitarians in this context), however, have a different interpretation of what kind of thing the common good is. That view starts with a denial of social (and metaphysical) atomism and insists that groups, organizations, communities are also included in the furniture of reality. What is good for, say, a given family may not even be recognized by, much less preferred by, any member of that family.

At this point very treacherous waters are drawing near – it is possible here to start drawing very totalitarian conclusions from the claim above, conclusions certainly not those of the progressive tradition. How one reasons in detail about the common good is beyond the purposes of this piece.

It is enough for my purposes to have pointed out that there are adequate justifications available for employing the notion of the common good as a way of successfully defending some particular restriction on people's freedom to act as they will. That is a lesson about liberty that needs to be learned by the radical right.

Lessons in Liberty (Part 6): Freedom – and Vaccinations

A man named Jacobson filed suit in opposition to a Massachusetts law requiring vaccination against smallpox. The case made its way to the Supreme Court where it was decided in 1905 by a 7-2 vote with Justice John Marshall Harlan writing the decision. The Court's conclusion was that the state did have the power to require vaccinations for the common good. From the decision:

"The defendant insists that his liberty is invaded when the State subjects him to fine or imprisonment for neglecting or refusing to submit to vaccination; that a compulsory vaccination law is unreasonable, arbitrary and oppressive, and, therefore, hostile to the inherent right of every freeman to care for his own body and health in such way as to him seems best, and that the execution of such a law against one who objects to vaccination, no matter for what reason, is nothing short of an assault upon his person.

"But the liberty secured by the Constitution of the United States to every person within its jurisdiction does not import an absolute right in each person to be, at all times and in all circumstances, wholly freed from restraint. There are manifold restraints to which every person is necessarily subject for the common good. On any other basis, organized society could not exist with safety to its members. Society based on the rule that each one is a law unto himself would soon be confronted with disorder and anarchy. Real liberty for all could not exist under the operation of a principle which recognizes the right of each individual person to use his own, whether in respect of his person or his property,

regardless of the injury that may be done to others. This court has more than once recognized it as a fundamental principle that "persons and property are subjected to all kinds of restraints and burdens, in order to secure the general comfort, health, and prosperity of the State, of the perfect right of the legislature to do which no question ever was, or upon acknowledged general principles ever can be, made so far as natural persons are concerned." [The court has previously said] "The possession and enjoyment of all rights are subject to such reasonable conditions as may be deemed by the governing authority of the country essential to the safety, health, peace, good order and morals of the community. Even liberty itself, the greatest of all rights, is not unrestricted license to act according to one's own will. It is only freedom from restraint under conditions essential to the equal enjoyment of the same right by others. It is then liberty regulated by law."....

"Smallpox is known of all to be a dangerous and contagious disease. If vaccination strongly tends to prevent the transmission or spread of this disease, it logically follows that children may be refused admission to the public schools until they have been vaccinated. The appellant claims that vaccination does not tend to prevent smallpox, but tends to bring about other diseases, and that it does much harm, with no good.

"It must be conceded that some laymen, both learned and unlearned, and some physicians of great skill and repute, do not believe that vaccination is a preventive of smallpox. The common belief, however, is that it has a decided tendency to prevent the spread of this fearful disease and to render it less dangerous to those who contract it. While not accepted by all, it is accepted by the mass of the people, as well as by most members of the medical profession. It has been general in our State and in most civilized nations for generations. It is generally accepted in theory and generally applied in practice, both by the voluntary action of the people and in obedience to the command of law. Nearly every State of the Union has statutes to encourage, or directly or indirectly to require, vaccination, and this is true of most nations of Europe.

"A common belief, like common knowledge, does not require evidence to establish its existence, but may be acted upon without proof by the

legislature and the courts.

"The fact that the belief is not universal is not controlling, for there is scarcely any belief that is accepted by everyone. The possibility that the belief may be wrong, and that science may yet show it to be wrong, is not conclusive, for the legislature has the right to pass laws which, according to the common belief of the people, are adapted to prevent the spread of contagious diseases. In a free country, where the government is by the people, through their chosen representatives, practical legislation admits of no other standard of action; for what the people believe is for the common welfare must be accepted as tending to promote the common welfare, whether it does, in fact, or not. Any other basis would conflict with the spirit of the Constitution, and would sanction measures opposed to a republican form of government. While we do not decide and cannot decide that vaccination is a preventive of smallpox, we take judicial notice of the fact that this is the common belief of the people of the State, and, with this fact as a foundation, we hold that the statute in question is a health law, enacted in a reasonable and proper exercise of the police power.

"Since, then, vaccination, as a means of protecting a community against smallpox, finds strong support in the experience of this and other countries, no court, much less a jury, is justified in disregarding the action of the legislature simply because, in its or their opinion, that particular method was -- perhaps or possibly -- not the best either for children or adults."

Note: The entire decision can be found
at https://supreme.justia.com/cases/federal/us/197/11/case.html

This decision (which happens to be about the present concerns with vaccination) presents a powerful argument that even in the United States freedom can be properly restricted for specific reasons. What is further interesting about it, given that the theme of this essay concerns reasons for restricting freedom, is that it employs along the way a variety of (seemingly) different reasons why freedom might be restricted in such a case as was being considered.

Let me note what reasons are mentioned: "for the common good", "injury to others", "general health, comfort and prosperity of the State", "safety, health, peace, good order and morals of the community", "common welfare".

Now some of those probably mean the same thing, are probably just linguistic variants of one and the same reason. But there are just as likely differences also. As I said earlier I do not intend to examine the entire (?) set of reasons that may be employed to justify opposition to the exercise of freedom in various kinds of case.

What I do want to point out is that each different reason can be subjected to critical examination to see whether it is a sufficient reason for restraining someone's freedom to act in a particular kind of case. The first reason mentioned in the Court's decision above, and one that frequently is employed in similar contexts, is that the restriction is "for the common good".

That has been rejected as a reason for government action by some thinkers. Next time, I will examine the reasons why it has been rejected and offer a defense of its employment.

Notice that a new question comes up at this point. Suppose someone were to attack that line of argument which involves an appeal to the public good, the public welfare, by holding that there is no such thing as the public good.

Let me jump to a much less important case. The Congress not long ago passed standards for light bulb efficiency that in effect will prevent the sale of incandescent bulbs for general lighting purposes. There was a huge outcry against that act (and there remains opposition.) There were/are several grounds for that opposition - e.g. fears of mercury poisoning, greater cost of the new bulbs, inferior lighting quality of the new bulbs and others. The only ground for complaint that is relevant here has to do with freedom: many who opposed the new law did so because it interfered with the freedom of consumers to purchase whatever kind of light bulbs they wished. The government had, on this complaint, wrongly interfered with freedom.

There is no doubt that it was a restriction on freedom. The question of course is whether it was/is a justified restraint on people's ability to pursue what they want.

Well, what did the Congress and other advocates of the law have in mind as the reason for phasing out old style bulbs and setting standards that broadly require elimination from the market and thus from places where general lighting is used of incandescent bulbs?

The Hippocratic Oath

My wife tells me that her hairdresser has been encountering doctors who say that 'Obamacare' will be a disaster. Why they say that seems to involve a confusion between their self-interest and the public good. The disaster that they foresee is that they, correctly, expect a hugely increased case load when all the new insurees are in the fold – and of course there will be lots of them since so many of our fellow Americans have been shut out of health insurance. For the doctors a larger case load means more mistakes. And more mistakes mean they will be sued more frequently than they presently are.

Now one can feel some sympathy for the doctors. Until, that is, one recalls that their way of putting it, that 'Obamacare' is a disaster, is not a fair judgment about the merits of the new law, but is merely a projection of their own problems onto the ACA overall.

And then one also realizes that the doctors, and their professional organizations, have been complicit in the current system and so are, in part, morally responsible for its short-comings, short-comings that will be partially rectified by the new law. Doctors and their professional organizations could have seen beyond their own self-interest to the well-being of the American public and insisted upon a system that made health care available to all. That would have required allowing for more doctors, especially in primary care, for utilizing other medical professionals more extensively in treatment, for thinking of better ways of delivering health care than the current system provides.

The Hippocratic oath, some version of which most American doctors still must subscribe to, is a relic of an ancient way of organizing medical care. It focuses attention on the individual doctor's relation to the individual patient and encourages a short-sighted view of how medical practice relates to an entire population.

The Hippocratic oath needs to be redone in light of changes in the world in the last 2500 years.

Proverbs and Food Stamps

It is said that the devil can quote scripture for his own purposes. But the really curious thing is how the faithful (the ascendant branch of American Christianity that is) can refuse to quote scripture when the omission suits their own purposes. Charity requires treating that as a case of blindness, not cynicism.

How many fundamentalist preachers have quoted from the pulpit or on their television shows the following: Proverbs 29:7 "The righteous care about justice for the poor, but the wicked have no such concern." Or Proverbs 14:31 - "He who oppresses the poor shows contempt for their Maker, but whoever is kind to the needy honors God." Or Proverbs 22:16 - "He who oppresses the poor to increase his wealth and he who gives gifts to the rich – both come to poverty. "How many of the Christians in the House of Representatives reminded their fellows of those proverbs during the debate on food stamps – or at any other time in recent memory?

Those failures might even lead those of other faiths and those without any religion to think that that particular bunch of Christians are either ignorant of their own holy writings or are not really believers in that form of religion, are in fact CINO's.

Two Cheers for the Affordable Care Act

I am very tired of hearing all the phony and often absurd criticism of the Affordable Care Act. So I'm writing to praise it.

Keep in mind what "it' is. "It" is not the troubles with the Federal website, Healthcare.gov . Those problems are the result partially of normal difficulties in starting up a complex system, made more complex and difficult intentionally by 36 Republican-controlled states that, for anti-Obama reasons, refused to start their own sites, thereby over-loading the national site, and partially of a failure of proper oversight by the Obama administration. Nor is the "it" the cancellations of inadequate insurance and Obama's inexplicably mistaken claim that there would be no cancellations. Cancellation of junk policies was always an aim of the ACA, but it has been made worse by

insurance companies' premature and unnecessary cancellations in the interest of misleading people into more expensive policies. Criticism of the ACA on either of those grounds is irrelevant to an evaluation of the Act itself.

I do not intend, in praising the Act, to run through a very long list of its good things. Those can be found in any competent assessment of it. Rather I wish to assert here a very simple claim: the ACA is one of the most monumentally valuable creations of our government.

It is not the best that could have been done: a single-payer system, similar to Medicare for everyone, would have been far superior. Second best would have been the present ACT if it included a 'public option', allowing people of all ages to buy into Medicare. But in trying to save the primary role of private insurance companies in the US health care system, Senator Max Baucus (the Act should be called Baucuscare in recognition of its chief architect) settled for the third best outcome.

Nonetheless, the ACA is such a huge step forward, another step in the long attempt to move our health care system to what all the other developed countries have long since achieved, to a system in which everyone is granted as a matter of right access to healthcare. The ACA does not get us all the way there: but it is, given political realities, a giant moral advance, giving us a decently respectable place in the community of nations.

Everyone of good will is rooting for the quick success of the ACA and hoping that its flaws will be corrected in the near future. If you are instead hoping for failure of the Act, you simply do not appreciate what the ACA is going to do for every American and thus for the country.

Let us have two cheers for Obamacare.

On Being Addicted to Your Own Welfare

The anti-government faction in this country thinks of people's liking for Medicare and Social Security as an addiction, as a goodie craved by those with a social sweet tooth. In the same way they express their fear that once the Affordable Care Act fully comes into play people will also become 'addicted' to it; hence it must be stopped, repealed, before people get a taste of it, before the craving captures them.

That those social programs are thought of by the right as irrationally appealing is not surprising. The libertarians in their opposition to government conceive of themselves as fully rational (their chief publication is named *Reason*) and so they are faced with the task of explaining why people are attracted to what seems to libertarians as people's irrational longing for government to play a role in their lives, to help make their lives better.

We liberals must then be thought of as the political equivalent of drug dealers. That we rationally defend Medicare and so on as working for the common good, that we argue for the existence and expansion of the social safety net as morally desirable for living more fully human lives, that we reject the libertarian arguments for their shrunken conception of life, cannot be mentioned in the public sphere by libertarians. And that people come to see, whether on the basis of argument or on the basis of experience, that we are right, that their and their fellow citizen's lives are improved by the safety-net programs, cannot be accepted by the right as a rational conclusion.

Hence they have resort to the language of addiction as the only way to make sense of the situation. We, on the other hand, both those who advocate such programs and those whose lives are improved by them, must be treated as drug-dealers and druggies.

Equality and the Declaration of Independence

The conservatives, given their total commitment to freedom as *the* political value, read the Declaration of Independence as nothing more than an assertion of freedom.

What they ignore is that while the Declaration announces and justifies the claimed freedom of the colonies from British rule, it does not otherwise treat freedom as the sole, not even the major, value for the people of the colonies.

The Declaration opens with a brief paragraph noting that the colonies were in this document declaring themselves free from the political bonds that tied them to Britain. It goes on to say that an explanation and defense of breaking away from its mother country is needed. In the 2nd paragraph, the Declaration begins that explanation.

It opens with words familiar to Americans: "We hold these truths to be self-evident, that all men are created equal...." What is so widely overlooked, especially by conservatives espousing freedom in every aspect of life, is that when the time comes to defend the act of declaring political freedom, the very first thing that is said in that defense rests upon the natural <u>equality</u> of all men. It is implied that remaining under British rule would not allow the colonists to achieve the natural state of equality with each other and with others. Hence independence, self-rule, is declared.

What form of political life is suitable for a people committed to idea that all men are created equal? Obviously a democracy.

It took more than a decade that included a war to achieve independence and a failed try at a workable political arrangement before the founders established a Constitution that satisfied them as roughly meeting the requirement that everyone be thought of as equal. It is not easy, however, to be clear and certain what constitutes the translation of the fundamental thought that all men are created equal into practical, democratic terms. Only slowly did we come to see that more was required than the founders realized. Slavery had to be overcome – women had to acquire political rights – and several other developments were necessary (and there are other conditions that have not yet been realized in practice.) In short, we did not become a full democracy with the creation and acceptance of the Constitution.

In the attempt to express constitutionally the thought that we are equal, there was an issue over and above the failure to confront slavery and the place of women that largely escaped the founders. What should be done about the role of wealth in a democracy?

No doubt the founders did not deeply consider that problem for several reasons. They themselves were men of wealth and since they were trying to set out what makes for the common good, they assumed that wealth was not a major issue for a democratic government.

More importantly, wealth at that time was largely in land ownership. The wealthy owned land and the tools to work it – the poor did not. What they did not realize was that at the same time as we were becoming a country, there was a major change in the economic life of England and soon elsewhere. A new form of capitalism, industrial capitalism, was just getting underway in Britain. The nature of capitalism itself was not understood – the first great explanation of that type of economy – Adam Smith's The Wealth of Nations - was published in 1776, the same year as the Declaration of Independence.

Our founders, who had substantial knowledge about and interest in political theory and political history, they had no glimmer of modern economic life. There is thus nothing to be found in our Constitution about the economic system that was springing up in Britain and no thought given to the possibility that the great wealth created by modern capitalism would cause problems for the asserted equality of men and the democratic form of government that was being created to achieve that equality.

Thus we today cannot look to the founders and to our basic political document for guidance on how to maintain the fundamental assumption that we are equal. And it is surely obvious that from the Gilded Age (say 1890 to 1933) that vastly increasing wealth, and the power it confers, has been the chief tension in our political and economic lives. Today we have reached a state of inequality among our citizens that rivals that of the Gilded Age, undermining the assertion of the Declaration of Independence that all men are created equal. That circumstance was temporarily improved by the election of FDR in 1932. But the resurgence of the plutocrats beginning about 1970 has overwhelmed that attempt to re-establish equality as a fundamental value of the country. The talk these days is about how far the country has lost its democratic character and become instead an oligarchy, a plutocracy. The next several years will make that the basic issue of our political lives.

On Having a Baby

Some segments of the right-wing flipped out over Chelsea Clinton and husband's announcement that they are expecting a baby this autumn. Most of the news about the wing-nut reaction is a derisive push-back against the idea that the pregnancy is planned to assist Hillary Clinton in her presumed campaign for the Presidency, an attempt to win the grand-mother vote.

But there is another theme in some of the right's reaction: that by announcing that they were having a baby, the Clinton's and like-minded liberals are contradicting themselves on the question of abortion. For the anti-abortion folk declare that the human fetus is a person and that it becomes a person at conception. They then hold that to talk of having a baby is to commit the speaker to their theory about the status of a fetus. Consequently, they hold that Chelsea Clinton and her husband who, it is presumed, hold that abortion is acceptable, must in their talk of having a baby contradict their view about abortion. Only if they had said 'fetus' would they be home free and clear from the charge of contradiction.

I have no idea what words Chelsea and husband used in making the announcement (or elsewhere) except that it is extraordinarily unlikely that they used the word 'fetus'. They may have said 'We are having a baby this fall' and 'The baby is due in (say) October.' If so, there is not even the appearance of a contradiction: those words are prospective and say nothing about the current state of affairs.

However, if what was said is 'The doctor says the baby is doing just fine', then one is talking about a baby in the here and now. And so about that one can see the anti-abortion conservative taking flight.

However, that way of talking has absolutely no theoretical commitment at all. To think that it does would be like holding that anyone who says 'The sun rose at 6 am' or 'The sun swiftly sank below the horizon' is committed to the astronomical theory that the sun goes around the earth. It simply cannot be inferred from the use of those words what views about the relation of the sun and the earth a person holds.

Of course our talk about the sun rising and setting developed when people did believe that the sun moves and the earth is stationary. But we continue to talk in the old way even when we know that it is the earth's motion not the sun's that produces the appearance and thus the talk of the sun moving across the sky. The words presently used simply carry no theoretical commitment. So too, talking of how the baby is doing during pregnancy no doubt developed when there was a different reigning theory of the status of the fetus. But the language of babyhood to talk of the state of a fetus does not today commit a person to that religious theory about the commencement of personhood. It is a remnant of an older view but, just as in the case of the sun, we have divorced the words from a commitment to theories.

(Note: Does saying 'We are going to have a baby' commit the speaker to some wild biological views about simultaneous male and female pregnancy? Of course not.)

Cost of Free Riding

Health care free riders do not have insurance and use emergency rooms for service. Since hospitals must treat people who appear on their doorstep but get only about 10% reimbursement for what it costs them to treat the uninsured, the rest of us pick up the tab for the treatment in higher taxes and/or in higher fees for our own medical treatment.

So much has long been known. However, there is now a more precise and memorable number for how much medical free riders cost the rest of us. The Congressional Budget Office has estimated that in 2008 the uninsured shifted $43,000,000,000 (that is, $43 billion) worth of treatment costs to the insured.

Those who are calling for the repeal of the Affordable Care Act are either free riders or idiots defending free riding.

The Washington Taliban

The Taliban in Afghanistan dynamited some of that country's cultural treasures, the enormous 6th century Buddhas carved from the cliffs in the Bamiyan valley.

The conservative contingent in the current House of Representatives is the American Taliban: they want to destroy (among other things) NPR and PBS, American cultural treasures. They don't use dynamite: eliminating federal funding is their preferred method.

Fundamentalists world-wide are alike.

Requiring Health Insurance

In 1994 Kentucky (in those pre-Rand Paul days that state must have had some sense) required insurance companies to insure anyone without regard to pre-existing conditions, as our new Affordable Care Act does. But the Kentucky law did not require anyone to purchase insurance (the 'mandate'). As a consequence, many Kentuckians waited until they needed medical treatment, then purchased insurance – a variant form of free riding. As a result, insurance costs rose so much that insurers dropped out of the Kentucky market and the state was forced to repeal the law.

Massachusetts on the other hand (good ole Mitt Romney) instituted both the provision that everyone in Massachusetts is insurable no matter what their antecedent medical condition and the mandate. As a consequence, insurance premiums there have dropped 40% at the same time as the national average has gone up 14%.

Huge cheers for the mandate.

Speeding Up Marx

It is difficult to contradict oneself within the space of two sentences but Grover Norquist, in his best-known remark, has done so. "I don't want to abolish government. I simply want to reduce it to the size where I can drag it into the bathroom and drown it in the bathtub." If one wants to drown government in the tub that certainly seems to be getting rid of it. However, that contradicts his first sentence where he says he doesn't want to rid us of the 'evil'.

Marx, Engels and Lenin spoke of "the withering of the state". When the proletariat were well entrenched in power and the slogan 'From each according to his ability, to each according to his need' was fully operational, the state would fade from existence. Norquist, a hero to the right, cannot wait for the state to wither in some fuzzily distant future: it must be put out of its miserable existence pronto.

You the Master

As you read the following from Ludwig von Mises, that unbending advocate of the free market, seriously ask yourself whether you feel that you have the power and the mastery that he ascribes to us as consumers.

"In [a market economy] the entrepreneurs and capitalists are the servants of the consumers. The consumers are the masters, to whose whims the entrepreneurs and capitalists must adjust their investments and methods of production. " (von Mises, *Omnipotent Government*, pp. 49-50)

Forget the Koch brothers and other billionaires: take a somewhat smaller target. When you walk into your bank, say the Bank of America, do you act, think and feel as if that branch of the B of A is your servant, that your whims will cause them to bend to your will? Or take something even less grand, say your local shoe repair store: does it cater to your every desire? Does the owner promise you everything and wake up in an anxious sweat if it looks as if the promise might not be fulfilled?

The libertarian free-marketeer defends a piece of propaganda in the slogan 'The consumer is king'. It is generated by sliding from a bit of economic theory (applicable to an economy where the capitalists are small scale and have no power) to a description in terms of human life. The libertarian loves the theory – progressives think of what life is actually like.

Liberty and Justice

We Americans all have learned the Pledge of Allegiance with its rousing final words "with liberty and justice for all". Focusing on those words is one, only one, way of understanding the nature of the current tea party outburst.

For the tea party folk and their organizational and individual fellow travelers, those words from the Pledge should be rewritten to say only "with liberty for all." If you listen carefully enough – and sometimes not much care is needed – you will hear that the only value the TP bunch has is liberty, freedom. They like to imagine themselves as William Wallace at the end of *Braveheart* as he is disemboweled by the English: shouting 'Freedom! Freedom!' Hear their speeches and read their writings: the old American ideal of justice for all is never mentioned.

Taxes and Warren Buffett

The conservatives' response to Warren Buffett's reminder that he and the other rich (especially the super-rich) are being under-taxed: well then, freely send the IRS the money you think you should be paying in taxes.

Once again conservatives fail to engage the progressive view of taxes and consequently of living in a modern democracy. In a democracy, the willingness to pay taxes is a recognition of being a member of a civilized social order. To (only) make charitable contributions to government would be to treat oneself as a completely self-contained being who has no moral and social responsibilities to anyone other than oneself.

The narcissism of the conservative view is astounding.

Something of a Hero

Jered Weaver of the Los Angeles Angels recently signed a five year contract extension for $85 million. He could have got a lot more by going into free agency and taking what the market would give him. (Neo-classical economics of course rates him as irrational for that decision.)

Part of his reason is worth noting: "If $85 million is not enough to take care of my family and other generations of families [note that] then I'm pretty stupid [i.e. irrational], but how much money do you really need in life?"

Would that the Wall Streeters learn to ask themselves how much they really need in life! If they can't ask that and decide properly, i.e. within the bounds of common sense, then it is up to the rest of us, though government action and tax policy, to see that the question is correctly answered.

On the other hand, even if he poses the right question, Weaver will after all be getting $85 million over those 5 years – most people have to do with a very great deal less over the course of their entire lives. How much do they really need?

Can You Spare a Billion Buddy?

The right-wing is always complaining of government 'handouts'. The phrase conjures up the picture of slipping a dime (or a buck on generous days) into the hand of the guy on the corner. The conservative, though, slips the word and the picture into criticism of the government for handing out (his and her) money to the undeserving (poor).

However where do the big time government handouts go? The Pentagon is the handout king – and favored companies and corporations (down at the heels fellows, struggling to get by) are the recipients.

Any Goodman: "Meanwhile, the Pentagon's use of no-bid contracts has tripled since the United States was attacked on 9/11, in spite of promises to reform the controversial practice. According to a new investigative report from the Center for Public Integrity, no-bid spending has ballooned from $50 billion in 2003 to $140 billion in 2011." Now that's really handing it out, slipping the undeserving the odd billion.

For much more on the practice
see: http://www.democracynow.org/2011/9/2/

The Shot Heard Round the Internet (and Further)

Elizabeth Warren – mark that name; she is already being touted as the prime Democratic candidate for 2016 - vigorously set out a fundamental piece of progressive outlook and did so in a memorable fashion. What she had to say is a litmus test for being a progressive.

"I hear all this, you know, 'Well, this is class warfare, this is whatever. No. There is nobody in this country who got rich on his own — nobody. "You built a factory out there? Good for you. But I want to be clear. You moved your goods to market on the roads the rest of us paid for. You hired workers the rest of us paid to educate. You were safe in your factory because of police-forces and fire-forces that the rest of us paid for. You didn't have to worry that marauding bands would come and seize everything at your factory — and hire someone to protect against

this — because of the work the rest of us did.

"Now look, you built a factory and it turned into something terrific, or a great idea. God bless — keep a big hunk of it. But part of the underlying social contract is, you take a hunk of that and pay forward for the next kid who comes along."

She clearly hit a nerve. For speaking the truth she has been vilified by major conservative pundits: Rush Limbaugh, George Will, Jonah Goldberg. For an excellent critical analysis of Will's attack on her and thus on the progressive outlook see E.J. Dionne's *Refuting Straw Liberals*.

It's My House, Mine I Say

Those living near our southern border are likely to have encountered the welcoming saying 'Mi casa es su casa' (to those without simple Spanish 'My house is your house'.) The motto has a place in our politics, even if its authors and promoters do not notice it. Liberals apply 'Mi casa es su casa' to all Americans (not so enthusiastically to the rich among us) and even more broadly to those who have made their way into our lives (and often into our actual casa) without benefit of legal recognition: see support for the Dream Act. Conservatives are appalled by that. Their chief fear is that the poor of the earth have listened to the liberals and adopted a variant of the slogan, namely 'Su casa es mi casa'. So the conservative hangs outside his political door the plaque 'Mi casa is MI casa'.

They Want My Cadillac!

Today's conservative simply does not understand what people want. The protesters on Wall Street, to the conservative imagination, have no interest in the well-being of the country, are not motivated by the recognition that the high-flyers on Wall Street deeply damaged not just the US economy but the world's and did so out of greed, seeking nothing more than their own personal (monetary) interest. Not being able to see someone with motives other than their own, they attribute that outlook to the protesters. They are protesting out of greed, the desire to have what the banksters have. So Herman Cain: the OWS crowd are "jealous Americans", people who have not succeeded in the Great American Game and so are "playing the victim card" and, get this, people who want to "take somebody else's Cadillac"!

For the right, the protest is founded on nothing more than the principle: Su Cadillac es mi Cadillac.

(See http://www.latimes.com/news/politics/la-pn-cain-occupy-wall-street-20111009,0,972806.story)

Capitalism and Morality

It is often said that one of the beauties of capitalism is that moral considerations (are to) play no part in the decisions of the firm (nor for those of the consumer.) But that is precisely what makes it imperative that businesses be subject to regulations. Without regulations, capitalist firms are like a sociopath in the body social.

Authenticity and Tea Bagging

In the 1960's a colleague of mine gave a student's paper in an introductory philosophy class an F. The student came in to protest the grade. His justification for why the paper did not deserve an F: the thoughts were *his*. It had not crossed his mind that the grade was to be based on the quality of the ideas, the arguments and the presentation. Authenticity ruled!

Our current tea-baggers are the descendants of that student, of the spirit of the '60's (as much as they would hate to see those students as their ancestors.) Their protests are fervent, heart-felt. They are being authentic in what they say and feel and admire political figures (Bachmann, Cain, Perry) who say what looks to be authentically their own. The idea that thought, effort, and self-criticism are necessary to produce good political ideas has not crossed their minds.

Moreover, the thoughts really aren't their own. They fail to see that the movement is bankrolled by very very wealthy people who have been spreading these supposedly new ideas since the FDR era. The money-bags of the movement do not care a fig about the well-being of those shouting most loudly. They, in their drive for authenticity and lack of interest in thought, are being taken for a ride by an economic elite who are interested only in a political system that furthers their own well-being.

Again in the '60's, my department had a holiday party at which a graduate student slipped in, then out and left a dish of brownies – spiked of course with pot. The ensuing antics at the party were, to say the least, disjointed. The tea-party movement is not like a typical tea-party but rather like what happened to the unsuspecting pot-consuming party-goers: incoherent thought produced not by themselves but by someone who stayed well away from the mischief.

Money is Speech: Thought Experiment

Try this: imagine writing an intelligent letter on some topic of current interest to your elected representative; then imagine writing a letter expressing somewhat more crudely a contrary view but enclosing a $5000 check designated for the representative's campaign fund. Ask: which of the two will have the most impact, which is the more powerful speech from the representative's point of view? Money is not speech: it is (among other things) a means of getting attention to speech.

Scales Dropping from One's Eyes

Having epiphanies is not a frequent occurrence so it should be reported that Naomi Klein's piece on global warming in <u>The Nation</u> (a precursor to a book) has had that effect on me. For long I have simply said that the conservative denial of global warming is plain irrational. But Klein made me see that their view is a (partly) intelligible mixture of reason and madness. She holds that what the conservatives see, more clearly than progressives, is that if the earth is warming as the scientists and liberals say it is and if we must therefore act to slow it (or whatever is possible), one of the rational consequences is that the very ideology of contemporary conservativism must go out the window. Acting to stop/slow global warming will require a massive revision of our economic system and a corresponding large increase in government intervention in our economic lives. The conservative is thus caught between the case for global warming and their entire outlook. The irrationality comes in because they choose the ideology and thus are forced to deny the undeniable, the facts.

A Plutocratic Principle

The formula Money is Speech is jargon that enables and encourages sloppy thinking. In a money economy, money is a <u>means</u> to all kinds of things (even if not everything), including speech - one has to spend money to buy a stamp to mail a letter to the editor of the newspaper in order to exercise the right to speech.

The crucial thing is that the slogan has a corollary that is the root of the problem with the Supreme Court decision. If Money is Speech, then it follows that the more Money you have the more Speech you are entitled to. That is not the principle of a democracy but of a plutocracy: the rich are entitled to more speech than the rest of us (and we, simply in virtue of our wealth, are entitled to more speech than the guy living in the LA Mission.) Now it may be that as a matter of fact in a society marked by inequality of monetary resources, those with more will have greater opportunities to speak than those with less. But that is a factual matter. What the Supreme Court has done is to erect as a matter of *principle* the foundation of a plutocratic political order. Those of us committed to democracy, and that includes the Constitution, will find the Court's principle abhorrent.

For the Love of Creative Destruction

Talk of creative destruction is flying around these days in the wake of Mitt Romney's presidential campaign. His firm, Bain Capital, engaged in creative destruction and he is proud of it.

I suspect that he and those who are chiming in on the side of creative destruction do not realize that the notion was Marx's (we progressives, however, will not thereby call them Marxists as they would were the shoe on the other foot). It was Joseph Schumpeter who invented the term while working out Marx's notion – and Schumpeter, like Marx, thought that indulging in it would lead to the demise of capitalism. It is to be expected that those on the right do not attend to that feature of Schumpeter's argument.

Super PACs

Some memorable stats on Super PAC contributions:

In the previous two years a little less than 200 very rich people (think 1%) contributed about $90 million to Super PACs. Were you one of them?

93% of itemized contributions to those Super PACs were in amounts of $10,000 or more. Can you afford that? Can you even conceive of that?

37 people gave $500,000 or more. I suspect that you weren't one of those 37 people.

Sheldon Adelson and wife by themselves gave $10,000,000 to a single Super PAC.

See: <*http://www.demos.org/publication/auctioning-democracy-rise-super-pacs-and-2012-election*> and<*http://www.bloomberg.com/news/2012-01-25/adelson-s-10-million-pac-bet-gives-gingrich-boost-for-southern-primaries.html*>

The Tea Party and *Braveheart*

A few issues ago I proposed that the Tea Party people think of themselves as William Wallace as depicted by Mel Gibson in *Braveheart*: dying at the hands of the political authorities while shouting 'Freedom!'. My guess has been confirmed. It turns out that during the end-of-the-year House debate on the deficit, several of the right-wing representatives fired themselves up by watching *Braveheart* in a conference room. It was their equivalent of a locker room speech, a 'Win one for the Gipper' moment. Of course they, like Wallace's Scots, were slaughtered – but it was by vote not by sword. See the Dana Milbank piece in the Washington Post: http://www.washingtonpost.com/opinions/braveheart-republicans-or-false-hearted/2011/12/20/gIQA2Rxz7O_story.html

Is it Possible that Money Corrupts?

In the still developing response to the evils of the Citizen's United decision most of the criticism has focused on the Corporations are Persons and the Money is Speech principles used by the Supreme Court (in a 5-4 vote) to justify its decision making unlimited money available to subvert democracy. But recently much more attention has been paid to another aspect of the decision: the claim by the majority of the Court that a corporation that spends millions and millions of dollars to elect a candidate will not be a corrupting influence on the office-holder's political positions. The Five presented exactly no factual evidence to support that thesis: and common sense says that it is plainly false.

Ayn Rand and Ethical Egoism

The great popular heroine of the libertarian movement, Ayn Rand, espoused a doctrine called Ethical Egoism. It is not to be confused with Psychological Egoism which is the idea that we humans do, as a matter of our nature, act only for our own self-interest. Ethical Egoism finds, along with many others, that of course we can do things not generated by self-interest – but it insists that what we are morally required to do is only what is good for ourselves. Other people don't count morally. They of course may help or hinder us in our self-centered projects and so must be taken into account, but not as having any moral standing themselves.

To call the doctrine 'Ethical' is madly mistaken. Egoism is to be contrasted with morality – the moral perspective requires that it is the good of others that must be taken into account when working out the right thing to do. The name 'Ethical Egoism' is an attempt to claim the moral high ground when in fact it is a denial of morality. It is not the moral 'should' in the thesis that we should pay attention only to number 1 – it is like the 'should' in 'The shortstop should be playing more to his left': the shortstop who does not position himself to his left is not failing morally but is failing to be effective. To claim that people should act only in their own self-interest is to urge people only to be more effective as egoistic agents.

Deep Confusion About 'Government Handouts'

Susan Mettler (Cornell University) has conducted a study that reveals how confused the American public is about what a government program is. It turns out that 44 percent of Social Security recipients report that they "have not used a government program". So too say 43 percent of those receiving unemployment benefits and 40 percent of those on Medicare.

These people must think that 'government programs' are directed to people other than themselves, specifically to the idle and undeserving poor. Disliking such programs, they then condemn government generally ignoring the fact that they themselves are the beneficiaries of our social conscience. Through their confusion they put themselves in the pocket of the wealthy (the 1%) who have other (self-interested) reasons for condemning government.

To see an astonishing graph of Mettler's findings, to see how people over a range of government programs think that these are not government programs, see
http://www.news.cornell.edu/stories/March11/ChartLarge.jpg

Free and Fair

It has been one of my themes here that a pair of American ideals are captured at the end of what all of us learn as children, the Pledge of Allegiance: "with liberty and justice for all". However, just because they are ideals doesn't mean that they and we are in for smooth sailing: for often enough they (like other ideals) come into conflict.

And frequently enough we have to limit freedom in specific ways because some free acts do harm, are unfair, to another. Your freedom to take my apple is blocked because of the unfairness to me of your doing so no matter what your size or income.

In their first speeches when it became clear who the two American presidential candidates would be, each appealed to one of those ideals. One talked about freedom over and over, citing instances when the present administration encroached on freedom. Of course, what was ignored was whether those limits placed on liberty were justified restraints in the interests of justice. The current president talked about fairness, about giving everyone a fair shot. He of course did not talk about how some people's freedom to do as they wish must therefore be blocked in certain situations in order to ensure justice for all.

It would be wonderful to have this presidential campaign have an as an <u>explicit</u> theme those American ideals and how and when they come into conflict. It isn't to be expected though.

Religion in the Market

The flap over whether hospitals owned and operated by religions, including those that oppose birth control, should be required to offer contraception services as part of the medical insurance for their employees reveals much incomprehension on the part of the religious institutions, the media and the broader public.

For an example of that failure to grasp the issues see the following remarks from Father Paul Scalia, a parish priest in Virginia and son of Supreme Court Justice Antonin Scalia. Fr. Scalia thinks that the analogy between the HSS requirement and the case of Thomas More in the 16th century is "striking and instructive": More was put to death by Henry VII for refusing to accept the King as head of the church in England. The present American administration did not propose, not even remotely suggest, that it is head of the church. Again Scalia: "The crisis now before us between the bishops and the administration turns on the rights of the Church and the rights of man: the Church's right of self-governance and the rights of individual conscience. Since the mandate is imposed not only on Catholic institutions, but on all providers of employee health insurance, the individual Catholic as private citizen will suffer the injustice of this law. Just as Thomas More was not left unoppressed, neither will the individual Catholic be today. He too can be made to violate his conscience by conformity to this ruling." That is a cousin of, and as misguided as, the idea that regulation of business activity is socialism. The possibility of a fine for failing to provide the contraception provision in insurance is said by Fr. Scalia to be "In effect, a fee to be Catholic." Hogwash!

Fr. Scalia, the protesting religious institutions and their friends fail (refuse?) to see that churches, by putting themselves in the marketplace by operating public hospitals, are removing themselves from the religious arena in which their religious views are protected speech and thought. If those hospitals hire people not of their own religious persuasion, then they are engaging in market behavior and are to be governed by rules of the market-place. And the rules are that there must be no discrimination on the basis of religious orientation – which is what denial of contraception coverage for their employees outside their religion amounts to.

Moreover, as with all hospitals today, those hospitals receive federal monies. That makes them subject immediately to federal regulations. To receive federal funds and yet to claim exemption from public rules on the grounds of religious belief would be to violate the principle of the separation of church and state.

To claim, as was so often done, that requiring the coverage would be an attack on religion shows a complete lack of comprehension of the nature of our system. Of course, it might simply show that you can try to get away with whatever you can get away with without regard to political and moral principles.

Teachers: The Great and the Average

We chuckle when Garrison Keillor tells us that all the children in Lake Wobegon are above average. However, we fail to recognize the similar ridiculousness when we are told that all the teachers in our public schools should be great. No one plans for an educational system in which the teachers are average.

Of course, an increase in salary and status (in this country those are nearly but not quite the same thing) would raise the average quality of teachers. But then those who urge having only above average teachers don't want to indulge in that straight-forward piece of improvement. Of course, if that were done, teaching staffs would still mainly consist of average teachers.

Gay Marriage and The Religious Right

There are no secular objections to contraception and to abortion. Are all the objections to gay marriage also religious? If a gay couple has children, however acquired, then I think there might be some secular worry about the effect on the children of not having parents of different sexes in the family. (I think that the evidence shows, on the contrary, that there is not a significant effect on the children of same sex parents.)

But that problem arises not about the marriage per se but about children. Is there, then, any secular objection to the marriage status of same sex couples itself? No.

So once again all the flap about gay marriage arises only from a segment of the population – and it is not the religious segment as that is divided on the issue – which holds some ancient prescriptions about human sexuality. Progressives, religious and secular, need to keep pointing that out since the media seems not to catch on.

The Undeserving Rich

Stretching back into Victorian times, the right has made a distinction between (what they call) the deserving poor and the undeserving poor. What those phrases mean is not what they look to mean on the surface – the deserving poor are not the poor who deserve to be poor but are rather the poor who deserve outside assistance (charity is the chief means desired by the right) because their poverty is no fault of their own (think orphaned children left without family support.) The undeserving poor are those who do not deserve help either by welfare assistance (poor relief as it used to be called) or even by charity: their poverty is their own fault (with very generous fault lines.)

Conservative rhetoric and policy-making these days tends to ignore the (so-called) deserving poor: every recipient of welfare assistance is a welfare queen, someone who is scamming the system.

There is a hole in our vocabulary: the deserving rich and the undeserving rich are not categories we employ in public discourse. Of course, were such terms to come into use they would not parallel the terms about the poor: for the deserving rich would not be those in need of welfare assistance (though compare Tom Frank's <u>Pity the Poor Billionaires.)</u> Rather the conservative today talks as if all the rich deserve all their money while liberals have the suspicion that all the rich may be undeserving of <u>that</u> much of our economic resources.

Be They That Much Better?

In 2011 the median CEO salary in the U.S. was $9.587 million: a minimum wage worker in the U.S. would have to work 636 years to make that much - although a person making the national average salary would have to work only 244 years to achieve equality.

For more statistics about the wonders of our present system see: http://www.seattlepi.com/news/article/Top-CEO-pay-equals-3-489-years-for-typical-worker-3585109.php#ixzz1vwnwMq8H

Market Economies and Capitalism

I was amused the other day when reading a well-known (American) libertarian philosopher who tries to provide a moral defense of capitalism by talking of the glories of a market economy. Astonishingly he shares with the typical American the propaganda-induced idea that a market economy and capitalism are one and the same.

I own a home in New Mexico and receive my electricity from an electric co-operative. There is a market in electricity in the area and I chose to acquire mine from a non-profit consumer co-op rather than from the competing large for-profit, i.e. capitalist, corporation.

Anyone who thinks that markets and capitalism are identical should immediately trot down to their local credit union.

Texas: Oh Yes, It is Business Friendly

Politicians and people of the right frequently argue that states really ought to drop taxes, especially on businesses and the wealthy, in order to make their state more 'business-friendly'. If they don't, the argument goes, businesses will up and move to those states that are business-friendly.

However, is what is measured by those rankings of business-friendliness all there is to an evaluation of the quality of life in a state? Surely not.

Compare what else is true of Texas which ranks number one in the nation in business-friendliness and very high up the list of low tax states. The 2011 report 'Texas on the Brink' from the Legislative Study Group in the Texas legislature (Google it to see the entire report) compares Texas to all the other states in many categories of human well-being. In earnings of manufacturing workers Texas ranks 38th; it is 46th in percentage of residents who see a dentist; 1st in the number of executions; 50th in percentage of residents with a high school diploma; near last in SAT scores; 50th in air quality; 50th in water quality; 50th in percent of pregnant women who get prenatal care in the first trimester; 46th in percentage of children living in poverty; 49th in percentage of people with "food insecurity".

The account could go on and on. (See Gail Collin's recent <u>As Texas Goes...</u> for much more.)

Texas is, from the point of view of human flourishing, a failed state. But are they ever business friendly! Let's have all the states become low-tax, low service state so that they can become competitive with Texas.

Marriage Arrangements

One of the weakest arguments against same-sex marriage might be called the 'Antiquity and Ubiquity' argument. It holds that everywhere in space and time marriage has always been between one man and one woman. It of course doesn't follow that <u>we</u> really ought to be lemmings and do the same. But then it isn't even true that marriage has everywhere been an arrangement between one of each.

Anthropologists (and others) have recorded marriages consisting of one male with plural wives (strictly called polygyny but most often referred to as polygamy) as well as marriage between one woman and multiple males (polyandry).

If as a result of those facts, the original argument is defended by agreeing that the original premise was exaggerated but by claiming that everywhere and always within *our* tradition, marriage has been two people of the opposite sex, then the same result occurs. Supposing that our tradition is our Judeo-Christian heritage, then it is again false that that is what marriage has always consisted of. The *Bible* is replete with references to polygamous arrangements. (Check it out – try Google.)

It is very odd to see a Mormon defending the one man – one woman view of marriage given the polygamist history of the Mormon Church. Mormons dropped polygamy not in principle (the justification of the arrangement came from God after all) but in practice: it was abandoned simply because of the power of the Federal government and the hostility of the American public and not for reasons of principle.

In rejecting all the poly-forms of marriage, one might think that advocates of same-sex marriage would be praised for their acceptance of monogamy.

Pseudo Freedom

Libertarians, Texans (Governor Rick Perry named one of his boots 'Freedom' and the other 'Liberty') and Tea Partiers are wild about independence – of course it is their (not your) independence that they have in mind. But listen to the Pulitzer Prize winning novelist Richard Ford on kind of independence they have in mind. "It's this whole spurious idea of independence. The American practice of independence is premised on the notion of 'get away from me, because I'm better off when I'm here by myself...'; or 'my independence or my worth is more easily proven when I'm not somehow diluted by you...'. The whole way in which Western expansion or manifest destiny was lived out in American history is just the story of that: get away. Don't tread on me, or for that matter even get very close to me. Most of us have it in our make up; maybe it's human nature – Native Americans probably have it too, but it's particularly rife in the White American landscape. That's what my book <u>Independence Day</u> is about: the eventual sterility of cutting yourself off from liaisons with other people, from attachments, affinities, affiliations with other people. Finally the end of the line for independence is sterility." (<u>Conversations with Richard Ford</u>, edited by Huey Guagliardo)

The Wonder of Financial Success

Samuel Butler's 1872 satirical utopian novel <u>Erewhon</u> (an anagram of Nowhere) lays out (with tongue-in-cheek) the conception that the wealthy, both then and now, have of themselves. (You can also find this same conception in Ayn Rand and her libertarian offshoots.)

Erewhon: "This is the true philanthropy. He who makes a colossal fortune in a trade...and by his energy has succeeded in reducing the price of woolen goods by a thousandth part of a penny in the pound, this man is worth ten professional philanthropists. So strongly are the Erewhonians impressed with this, that if a man has made a fortune...they exempt him from all taxation, considering him a work of art, and too precious to be meddled with...saying 'How very much he must have done for society before society could have been prevailed upon to give him so much money.'"

Slogans

1960's slogan: Don't trust anyone over 30
2010's slogan: Don't trust anyone over $250K

Déjà Vu All Over Again: FDR 1936

"We have had to struggle with the old enemies of peace – business and financial monopoly, speculation, reckless banking, class antagonism, sectionalism, war profiteering. They had begun to consider the Government of the United States as a mere appendage to their own affairs. We know now that Government by organized money is just as dangerous as Government by organized mob."

What Liberalism Is

"The test of our progress is not whether we add more to the abundance of those who have much; it is whether we provide for those who have too little." (FDR Memorial, from 1937 Inaugural Speech)

The Successful Life

It has been widely recognized for some time that Americans tend to measure success in life by success in making money. That is probably an outgrowth of America's Calvinistic streak from the Puritans – the more success in business the greater the sign that God has given you salvation.

In some ways, that American ideal is a version of the Aristotelian idea that there is but a single measure of human happiness or flourishing. Of course Aristotle didn't think that it was money made (or possessed) but he did hold that lives could be measured by a single (if complicated) standard.

The liberal tradition rejects that notion. Each person must be understood as having, even if very vaguely defined, her or his own 'life project', what they want out of life. In this view success in life means how well a given person has been able to satisfy their own goals and aims. (There are problems with making that the whole story but let those remain for another day.)

Now someone might have a life project of making as much money as possible – and if they acquire a fortune, then their life has been a success by their own lights. But we have no right to hold to that standard for measuring another person's life success if it was no part of their scheme of things. Nor is there any plausible argument that we ought to have making a large amount of money a necessary part of any acceptable life project.

It never crosses the mind of the overwhelming majority of people, even of Americans, that they should devote their lives to the making of money.

Conservatives do not manage to notice that their idea of what we should try to attain in life contradicts their basic emphasis on individual freedom. Liberalism does it much better.

Makers and Takers

The favorite new conservative terminology for dividing Americans is to distinguish between makers and takers: those who contribute to the economy and thus pay taxes and those who make no contribution and are parasites on those who do by taking safety-net monies paid for by the work and taxes of the takers.

Liberal commentators have had a field day shooting down that conception of the takers, of the 47%. There are at most a handful of people who satisfy the conservative idea of the taker, those who could be working but don't because they are sponging. Others of the 47 percenters do pay taxes (not income tax) and work hard or are otherwise entitled to support for various reasons (people in the military, the disabled.) There is nothing of any significance left of the case for the conservative idea of the takers: many of those they so classify are themselves makers, people who work hard (typically very hard). What they fail to make is sufficient money though they are economic makers.

The other side of the coin has not been so well discussed: are those called 'makers' by the conservatives really makers? People who take nothing from the public? There is no such beast. People who make things that have no redeeming social value? There are plenty of those too.

The really well-off ones have learned to game the system even better than the largely imaginary poor pure takers – even ignoring the total infrastructure within which they operate (which they didn't build), so very many of them have acquired government handouts, have favorable tax breaks, produce objects not of social value (derivatives for example). The odds of there being pure makers in the country are as slim as the odds of the pure takers.

The conservative categories of makers and takers are useless for understanding what actually happens in the economic life of the country.

Fighting Off the Plutocracy

While analysts reflect on the recent election, there is one topic I have not seen discussed. The election blocked, for the time being at least, a major attack on American democracy. There were three components of that attempt to undermine the political character of the country.

First, political campaigns and governance always involve a tense relationship with truth. But as many commentators have pointed out, no previous presidential candidate so fully refused to accept truth as a value in democratic leadership. In this election, the Republican candidate rejected the importance of truth, of facts. The aim was solely to attain power no matter what the facts. A democracy cannot exist when its leaders, and would be leaders, have no regard for truth.

Second, the Republican Party, through a variety of tactics in the service of 'voter suppression', tried to prevent voting (and to some extent succeeded) on the part of people who were presumed to be likely Democratic voters. Studies have shown repeatedly that there is no significant amount of voter fraud in the country. Moreover, in a democracy the presumption must be that it is better to allow some who are not eligible to vote than to create conditions in which genuine citizens are prevented from casting their ballots.

Third, the huge amount of money spent in the campaign, unleashed by the Supreme Court's logically and historically unacceptable Citizens United decision, went (of course) overwhelmingly to Republican candidates. Corporations and the very rich were enabled by the decision and their wealth to try to further replace our democratic system with a plutocracy.

Fortunately, the attack this time was blunted: lying, voter suppression and excessive money spent did not succeed in electing the party of the rich and powerful. Only if we all become aware that this election was an onslaught by the wealthy against ordinary citizens and against our democratic values, can we hope to repel more class warfare in the future and also dislodge the gains it has already made while we slept.

Shall It Be Me or We?

Football coaches (and perhaps others too) are fond of reminding their players that there is no 'i' in 'team'.

Ayn Rand hated the message behind that ostensible spelling lesson: for her the only thing we should consider in life is 'i' or rather I.

I remember from years ago when I read <u>Atlas</u> <u>Shrugged</u> (why didn't it thrill me as it did Paul Ryan?) that a train wreck occurs in the novel and that one of the people who died, whose death Rand, at her most vicious, cheered, was a teacher who tried to teach her students the value of team work, of being a team player.

The problem is that there are, contrary to Rand, many occasions when it is to the good to subordinate one's own personal interests to a larger view (taxes should be raised, my own included). But it is also true that there are many times when it is not to the good to do so (voting for an attack on Iran's nuclear facilities because I will get a plum committee assignment or more votes from my constituents.)

There is no single solution – neither 'always' or the Randian 'never' – to the problem of when we should subordinate our own personal interests to the well-being of others. We all do know that. We just happen to live in a time when a spasm of libertarianism is encouraging regard for nothing but self, the Ego.

We're in This Together

The libertarian right likes to contrast themselves with us, with liberals, progressives, social democrats and leftists generally as having an individualist opposed to a collectivist outlook.

We, of course, never call ourselves, even think of ourselves, as collectivists. That word in this day calls to mind Stalinist collective farms and no one in their right mind thinks that we would like life to be lived like that. The Randian may think that our principles inevitably lead to such an organization of life, but that involves a complete misunderstanding of liberal views.

The term we might use of ourselves is not 'collectivist' but 'communitarian': for we do emphasize that we are connected to others, that we must recognize and appreciate that fact and might even wish to (freely) develop that aspect of our lives more fully. (That sort of version of how we should live is most fully expressed in the Israeli kibbutz – no doubt a horror to the libertarian also.)

The term 'collectivist' is also quite useless in descriptive political theory for it has been created by the right precisely to lump together enormously different strands of political thought and then to label them with a pejorative derived from Soviet practices. For as used by the right it covers both prescriptive totalitarian thought and views which only hold that we are in fact connected to one another. It is a libertarian fantasy that each man is, contrary to John Donne, an island.

The liberal tradition is one that tries to find a way to make a place for both - our lives together and individualism. It rejects both the totalitarian idea that the group is superior to the individual and that hence individuals must sacrifice (that is the favorite notion of Ayn Rand) themselves for the greater good and also the hyper-individualism of libertarianism. Working out the details of a satisfactory arrangement makes social democratic thought much more difficult than the simplistic certainties of either libertarianism or totalitarianism.

Note: shortly after I wrote this I saw the film <u>Late Quartet</u> (Phillip Seymour Hoffman, Christopher Walken, Catherine Keener.) It is about a world-class string quartet that has been together 25 years but is about to lose one of its members. The film is a brilliant exploration of the contrary pulls of community (in this case the quartet) and individual desires. It is an excellent reminder of the liberal attempt to take into account both sides of our nature, the need for co-operation and the search for one's own way.

Biggie

I read a conservative writer the other day arguing (as usual) that the U.S. government is too big – the reason he offered is that it is bigger (in terms of employment, etc) than the world's largest corporation.

The argument reminded me of a friend who (many years ago now) was the biggest player, at 6'4", on his high school basketball team. Unfortunately, that meant he had to guard the opposing team's center and his team had the misfortune of playing in the same league in Brooklyn as Power Memorial High School whose center was the young Lew Alcindor (later, of course, Kareem Abdul-Jabbar.)

It isn't the absolute size as the conservatives think: it is the size relative to the challenges to be faced. And the case can easily be made that the challenges we face in this country may well require a bigger government still. Although, if the military-industrial complex can be tamed and the correct challenges faced, the absolute size of the government might end up being smaller than today. But of course, the conservative is not complaining of the size of our military.

The Right to Own a Gun

Let me agree at the start that there is a constitutional right for individuals to own and possess guns. What in the Constitution produces that right is a different story, one for another time and place. This short piece will be about how to understand rights.

Having a right does not give one carte blanche freedom to exercise that right. If a male is hired to do janitorial work at the high school and thus has as part of his job the right to enter the girls' locker room to clean it, that does not give him the freedom to enter the locker room whenever he pleases. We licensed drivers have the right to drive down the main street of our town but that does not enable us to exercise that right during the local 4th of July parade. A full-fledged right to gun ownership is perfectly compatible with all kinds of regulations designed to provide for public safety.

One can, of course, lose a right: a person's driver's license can be taken away permanently and so the right to drive is lost. On the other hand, being sent to prison for a crime does not take away the person's right to liberty: it takes away their liberty for a period of time because of the commission of some offense. Regulations on gun ownership do not take away the right to own a gun or even guns. Like other rights, that constitutional right is, or can be, hedged about with restrictions designed to provide for public safety.

The President on Education

In his Second Inaugural speech, President Obama gave a serious place to the subject of the education of Americans. But, as typical, the conception of education informing his words was hardly suitable. He thinks of education as proper training so that the student can get a job. What he mentioned in the speech was science, math and technology. There is not a hint of anything more for our educational system to aim at.

Having the skills to work is a necessary aim of how we educate ourselves. But that aim must take its place amidst other aims. We need to provide an education in what it is to be a citizen of a democratic nation. We need to provide an education that shows students the possibilities of developing understanding of history and art and literature and philosophy.

Given his personal attainment and his values, Obama's conception of education is shockingly shallow – suitable for, say, George W. Bush

Small Businesses and the Affordable Care Act

As the next phase of the implementation of 'Obamacare' gets nearer, small businesses (very many at least) are crying about the difficulties of satisfying its requirements for providing their employees with health insurance. But progressives can go only so far in feeling sorry for them. For the organizations representing small businesses could have foreseen just these troubles and urged the Administration and Congress to support a far simpler and less burdensome to business means of providing health insurance, namely single-payer or 'Medicare for All'. Instead, by choosing to go with a scheme that enabled insurance companies to remain major players in providing health care (protecting capitalism and big bucks), they helped bring the deluge of new regulations upon themselves.

Of Arms and the Man (Justice Kennedy to be precise)

In order to move forward on gun regulation, we progressives need to stop arguing that there is no Constitutional right to gun ownership. Of course, we do not have to base that agreement on the 2nd amendment or to accept the very badly done decision by the Supreme Court in the District of Columbia v Heller case, a 5-4 vote with the majority opinion written by Justice Scalia that claims it is the 2nd amendment that gives that right.

As Constitutional scholars have argued, contrary to the NRA and to the Court majority, it is far more plausible to hold that it is the 9th amendment that provides a right to gun ownership. The text of the 9th is "The enumeration in the Constitution of certain rights shall not be construed to deny or disparage other rights retained by the people." It can be held that the right to have a weapon for hunting and defense was a matter of fact in the frontier society that was America at the writing of the Constitution and the Bill of Rights. (It went without saying.)

In the oral arguments in the Heller case, Justice Kennedy kept referring to such things as "the concern of the remote settler to defend himself and his family against hostile Indian tribes and outlaws, wolves and bears and grizzlies and things like that" and "the interests that must have been foremost in the framers' minds when they were concerned about guns being taken away from the people who needed them for their defense."

But as critics of the majority and Kennedy have pointed out, there is no evidence that those concerns had anything to do with the 2nd amendment but surely were what was in mind in writing the 9th: rights that were a matter of course in the American world at the founding and need not be mentioned specifically in the Constitution. Yet Kennedy never turned his thoughts to the 9th amendment and ended up supporting an implausible reading of the 2nd amendment.

Too Good to Pass Up

Conservatives claim that they want to cut 'entitlements', i.e. programs that provide things that people have rights to, in order to save money, to cut the budget deficit. They don't want to 'grow' the economy to provide more revenue and in a decent period of time balance the budget (or more) – rather they want to take away things that we have argued and convinced the country at large that Americans have a right to.

Since we are not going to give up on Medicare, as the right wants, they will nibble on it on the pretext that the nibbling will save money and help eradicate the deficit. They propose to do that by lifting the eligibility age from 65 to 67.

Now there are all sorts of reasons against doing that – a truly progressive recommendation would be that we lower the eligibility age, even to zero (Medicare for all.) But the ostensible reason for raising the age, saving money, is not a good reason. For the amount saved would be piddling in the face of our budget shortages.

Richard Eskow has proposed that conservatives, if they really want to save money, should emulate Jonathan Swift's 18th century advice in his satiric 'A Modest Proposal'. To solve the problem of hunger in Ireland, Swift 'recommended' that the Irish should eat their year old children: that would provide both a source of food and a lowering of the population allowing a greater share of other food for all. Eskow notes that the greatest health costs are in the last years of life. Hence if we <u>removed</u> Medicare coverage for those at the end of life we could both save the most money and even diminish the number eligible for coverage as people would die off faster.

Of course conservatives are not really interested in balancing the budget – they are interested in ridding ourselves of what the non-wealthy have a right to and to supply which requires that the wealthy must make significant contributions to. Since they can't eliminate that popular program they nibble at the fringes.

Creating Jobs

George had developed a successful small business repairing widgets. At the height of his success he employed 10 people in various capacities. The Great Recession squeezed people's desire to have their widgets repaired and so George had to lay off two of his employees.

Listening to conservative politicians and pundits during the 2012 election, George heard them say that small businesses (not government) were what creates jobs. George was impressed by the claim that he was one of those responsible for job creation in the American economy. Since job creation is desirable and since he was one of those whose role is produce new jobs and thus economic development, George decided (no doubt going off the rails) to perform this admirable role. So he rehired people to fill the two positions he had had to eliminate – and wanting to be good at his newly realized function of job creation, he added three more positions and hired people to fill them.

Alas, the market for widget repair had not improved much. George, having to pay additional wages to 5 workers without any additional business, soon ran his once successful business into the ground.

The moral, of course, is that employers should not, do not, think of themselves as job creators: they hire when the business is there, i.e. in response to consumer demand. Without that, they do not create positions or if they do so, as George, they are stupid in their line of work.

Of course, there are those employers such as Susan, who realize that there is an unfulfilled demand for what her company can provide and create jobs to satisfy it. But the moral is the same: the successful Susan is responding to demand.

Hence, whatever produces more demand for a good or service is what leads to job creation. That is what we need to focus upon. And that is what the government can do: create demand in times when it is weak.

Conservatives on the Safety Net

There are two conservative positions on a society having a safety net. The extreme position, the Randian version of libertarianism, is the death march: those who need

the safety net are the society's (read 'the economy's') losers and are completely expendable. In effect the Randians favor Kim Il Jung's version of Marie Antoinette: 'Let them eat grass'. The softer conservative line recognizes that not all those in need of a safety net are individually responsible for their plight. Those are the deserving poor. They should be given support while the undeserving poor might be supported out of compassion but only if any individuals are so inclined.

But who is to provide that support? Some of the (few) tender-hearted (nearly bleeding-heart) conservatives think that the state might set up minimal mechanisms to get the deserving poor back on their feet for another go at grabbing the brass ring. However, that is not the favorite line. The typical conservative thinks that the solution is to do what people have traditionally done to assist the down and out: it is not the state that should provide the help but rather families, churches (religious organizations) and even charities using funds given by whoever feels compassionate enough to contribute.

Liberals, progressives, social democrats reject that type of safety net. Well, they don't really reject it: we expect that families and charitable organizations should and will typically step up to help those in need. It is, however, the welfare provided by the state, by all of us in a democratic society, that holds the moral high ground for those on the left.

Why? Because we are excessively bleeding hearts? Because we love playing nanny? No. It is rather a matter of respecting the dignity of those in need that we should provide community assistance, not through the whims of individuals or private organizations but through the state as a matter of right. They are entitled to our help because they are part of our community. By providing that assistance in that way, through state aid rather than by charity, we do not make them dependent upon particular individuals for what they need. The right claims that we are producing dependent people by operating a state safety net – we on the other hand are working to free such people from dependency on the fluctuating good will of other people.

Not a Transformative Presidency

I received more than one appeal from White House staffers working to drum up public support for the attempt to keep almost all the Bush tax cuts from expiring at the end of the year. The request was that I submit an account of how a rise in my income tax of $2200 would affect my family.

I was strongly opposed to allowing the tax cuts to expire on the grounds of the harm that it would do to people and the economy. But I refused to submit any such story to the White House for use in its campaign to accomplish what I was in favor of.

Why? Because what was asked for was a story of how the rise in tax would affect ME. That is not, however, how the ending of those cuts for the 98% whose taxes would go up should be explained and defended. What is needed instead are lines of thinking about how the tax change would affect others, how it would harm all of us, how it would help throw the US economy into recession.

To treat the issue as one noticing how it affects oneself is to play into the conservatives' hands. That is their frame of reference: the individual's self-interest. For them there is no such thing as the public good. Thinking about other people is not part of their world.

The attempt of President Obama to obtain public support for a desirable policy by basing the argument on right-wing grounds might help carry the day in the short run. But it otherwise retains the status quo, enabling Americans to continue thinking only of oneself. Obama's presidency will thus not be transformative, not change American political life and thought in any fundamental way.

Note: I owe ideas and wording in the above to both Ricky Maslowski and Parkes Riley, good liberal thinkers both.

How to Read the Declaration of Independence on Equality in Today's World

Very often progressives appeal to the Declaration of Independence in support of the idea that one of our nation's fundamental principles is that of equality. There are, however, problems with pointing to that document to show that this country is founded on the aim of achieving equality. I do not mean the problems caused by the fact that not all people were treated equally at the time: slavery (most importantly) and the consequent self-deception about it are not the issues I have in mind.

The Declaration of Independence says "We hold these truths to be self-evident, that all men are created equal, that they are endowed by their Creator with certain inalienable Rights, including the right to Life, Liberty and the Pursuit of Happiness..."

It is quite clear that "created equal" was meant to say that the equality in status is given to everyone by "their Creator" and the Creator is to be understood as a divine being, God.

The problem is this: the Constitution established this country as secular and the Bill of Rights gave everyone a legal freedom <u>from</u> religion as well as a legal freedom <u>of</u> religion. And despite the fact that an individual's freedom from religion is not yet accomplished in American practice, i.e. we have not achieved the full legal secularization the Constitution calls for, in terms of fundamental law this is a secular country.

How can a secular America make use of the equality talk in the Declaration given that it is expressed in religious language? How can its talk of equality be made relevant today when it was originally given a religious backing?

It can be done. The Declaration does not have to be thrown on the trash-heap of history because what it says about equality was originally expressed by reference to a Creator God, a maneuver not later employed in the Constitution.

In today's secular terms, the Declaration is stating that in our laws and practices this country starts from a presumption of equality with the implication that divergences from equal status are what must be justified. America's fundamental commitment is to treat all human beings as having an initial equal moral standing.

The reference to morality means that certain inequalities are irrelevant to the aim of the Declaration and to our political lives: that we are not all equally good shortstops or mathematicians does not count as a criticism of the announced principle. It is only in case of morality, especially political/social morality, that the claim applies.

Contrary to the Declaration, this updating of what it says about equality is not to be treated as a truth: what we have in the Declaration is the expression of a *commitment*, not something that is either true or false. It has a different logical standing: *this* is how we are to regard people, namely as having equal status in our laws, policies and practices. And because it is not a truth, it is not self-evident: it is an announcement about how we are to proceed in our thinking and our actions.

69

The principle does not commit us to holding that people deserve the same moral standing no matter what they do. What people do can justify their losing the equal moral status with which they are endowed by our initial commitment to equality. That is, again, loss of equal status can be justified at least by what people make of their lives, by what they do and what they do not do.

However, what about the Creator language? It is very important that we today explicitly recognize that the Declaration was written at a time and place where that kind of reference was normal, in order to contrast ourselves with those who hero-worship the Founding generation. Unlike those who talk as if what the Founders said and thought are good for eternity, we progressives must hold *publically* that time passes, that some modes of talk and thought have changed in the course of our history. For instance, the Founders' ideas of the American economy do not begin to make sense in today's world.

So too their idea of how to express an American commitment to equality – in terms of a Creator and self-evident truths - is a reflection of the time and place of this country's founding and is not binding on us today. We have a different way of talking of such matters. It is the commitment to equality as a fundamental feature of our political lives that survives.

Note: the view expressed here clearly is a rejection of the doctrine of originalism found in debates about the Constitution. The original way of expressing the country's commitment to equality is of a different time and place and is not determinative of how we should understand the Declaration today.

The Wonder of Financial Success Again

"...if a man has made a fortune...they [the Erewhonians] exempt him from all taxation, considering him a work of art, and too precious to be meddled with...saying 'How very much he must have done for society before society could have been prevailed upon to give him so much money.'" (Samuel Butler, Erewhon, 1872) Butler does not mention how the works of art regard themselves. Today, it is not only our ordinary Erewhonians but even more strongly those who have amassed (or even inherited) a fortune, even those who have only a large annual income, think of themselves as so precious that we ought to reward them. However, the reward they think they are entitled to is not only exemption from taxation but the right to buy political influence without limit (see Citizens United.)

Solidarity: With Whom?

Angela Merkel told a Hamburg newspaper "There has already been voluntary debt forgiveness by private creditors, banks have already slashed billions from Greece's debt. I do not envisage fresh debt cancellation."

Merkel of course knows that the Greek economy is staggering (it is about 25% smaller than it was four years ago) under the weight of the loans from German bankers, knows that Greek unemployment is at 28%, with an astonishing 61% of Greek's under the age of 25 unemployed, knows the other human consequences of an economy in desperate straits.

But the bankers come first. They have given so much already.

Solidarity forever!

Transforming American Politics: Beware of the Inside Game

David Axelrod in his account of the Obama Presidency observes that Obama came into office hoping to transform American politics. But Obama's analysis of what needs to be changed and thus a clear idea of how to do that was quite mistaken.

It is not the gridlock in Congress that is the issue. That problem exists of course, but it is a consequence of the genuine problem: the American people are genuinely and deeply divided. They thus elect people to Congress who represent the divisions in the population and thus gridlock results in Washington. Consequently, unless the public is addressed and the differences in outlook made clear, the problem will not even be faced much less tackled. No amount of insider dealing in

Washington will work: Obama tried that and failed very badly.

Only a President who will explain to the American people our situation and defend a vision of what we need and lay out a program for achieving that has a prayer of starting to cease the gridlock. Only if that is done will enough voters be swung to support that set of values and the consequent program.

What was needed, and is still needed, to transform our politics is a President with a conception of the Presidency as a bully pulpit (TR) or who is willing to engage in some version of Fireside Chats (FDR). Rather than reaching out to the American people, President Obama thought that compromise with other Washington hands would change things. It didn't – and couldn't.

Re-organizing the States Ecologically

In the abstract, one might think that the two banks of a river have a great deal in common and that the people living on each side of the river might thereby share common interests. If so, perhaps they should be grouped together in the same political unit. That of course didn't happen in the case of say Louisiana and Mississippi where the Mighty Mississippi separates the two states – or again where the Columbia separates Oregon and Washington.

Conversely, why should political map-makers be so enamored of straight lines that at the Four Corners the perfectly straight boundaries of the adjacent states of Utah, Colorado, New Mexico and Arizona meet?

Suppose ecological thinking had been in the saddle when the state boundaries of the United States were decided? The map of the U.S. would look very different today.

John Wesley Powell, the soldier, scientist and great explorer of the American west, thought that the proper way of organizing political units, bringing people with common interests together, was based on watersheds. A state would be a watershed, "that area of land, a bounded hydrologic system, within which all living things are inextricably linked by their common water course and where, as humans settled, simple logic demanded that they become part of a community." He developed a political map of the west based on that ecological principle. That map can be found at

http://communitybuilders.net/wp-content/uploads/2013/09/Powell_Map.jpg

Even more fun is the extension to the entire United States of Powell's principle. Created by John Lavey this map even employs the actual names of states, re-organized to meet watershed requirements.

http://communitybuilders.net/wp-content/uploads/2013/10/Watershed_States-HI-RES.jpg

Are we likely to see a significant attempt to remodel the country to satisfy what would be the wisest plan ecologically? Of course not: the past has created too much to be overcome now. There have been and will be minor attempts to re-establish some boundaries (for example southern Oregon and northern California recurrently think of declaring their independence from current states and merging to form a new one but it hasn't happened and seems unlikely to do so.) But perhaps the realization that watersheds have common interests will lead to more regional co-operation, new political structures.

Re-distributing Wealth

The conservative has now, and has for long, screamed at programs, in fact at suggestions for programs, that redistribute wealth from those who have more to those who have not enough. In fact, it is the brave liberal these days who uses the word 're-distribution' in arguing that re-distribution programs are necessary for a healthy democracy and a healthy economy.

The conservatives 'conveniently' ignore that redistribution in fact occurs in the opposite direction, from those with less to those with more. For instance (and these are just instances) every tax cut for the 1% and every benefit cut to the working class redistributes wealth in reverse Robin Hood fashion. And don't say that those are not really redistributive programs – they are as much the results of government actions as is any liberal redistribution program (food stamps or minimum wage raise). There is flat out no difference except that the conservative, by making the very idea of redistribution a no-go zone, has succeeded in hiding the fact that reverse redistribution is taking place.

Conservative Nostalgia

It is one of the plaintive cries of today's right-wing that they want *their* country back. This nostalgia for our past is quite astonishing. For it requires, at best, an extremely selective memory of how things were.

Someone has listed a few of the important features of this country in the past. It was a country that publically engaged in lynchings and murders of blacks. It was the country in which union demonstrations were attacked by police, both public police and those hired by corporations. It was a country in which women were stay-at-homes, cooking, cleaning, raising kids, following the husband's orders. It was a country in which homosexuality was a crime, where homosexuality was hidden deep in the closet. It was a country in which segregation prevented blacks from mingling with whites, at lunch counters, in beds, in schools. It was a country in which Native Americans were dispossessed of their land and their culture. And on and on (not that all of those features of American life have now vanished.)

Notice, however, it is not that the conservatives want back our past – they want back *their* past. They want back the past when their kind of people ruled, when the arrangements described above were established by people who looked like and thought like they do now. The social conservative especially sees that they are losing power and that is at the heart of their nostalgia.

Progressives don't want their country back. They want a better one.

When is it Equal?

Consider this problem – which I am not inventing.

Suppose that we believe in equal treatment. I make (say) $30k per year and when I get a parking ticket for staying in one spot too long I am fined (say) $50. You, who make $100k per year, over-parked just as I did and so receive the same ticket and pay the same fine.

Is that equal treatment?

There is no correct answer to that question deriving solely from the concept of equality. For the fine is equal in amount for exactly the same infraction. So it is possible to hold that therefore we have received equal treatment. On the other hand, the fine is about 2% of my annual income and only .5% of yours; therefore, the pain caused by the fine is much more severe for me than for you for exactly the same infraction. That means that we are not being treated equally: my punishment is more severe than yours.

Hence a good case can be made for each form of punishment being what equal treatment would amount to.

That being so, how should we decide what is the best way of assessing the fine, a way that settles the question of equal treatment in the better of the two ways? The concept of equality cannot by itself settle that question. To do so requires a broader framework. There are two different frameworks, each of which solves the problem in the same way.

If we treat punishment not simply as retribution, as recompense for having done something wrong, but also as a deterrent to future acts, then clearly fining both persons an equivalent amount will not deter the person with a lot more money nearly as much as it does the person paying a higher price in terms of overall suffering. In the above case, the person making $100K per year can afford 4 similar parking tickets before being caused an equal amount of suffering as the person making $30K. Being fined the same amount is not nearly as much a deterrent for a person making a lot of money. (We know those kinds of case frequently happen.)

The conclusion, based on the aims of punishment, is that the amount of the ticket ought to be an equal percentage of income (or wealth) rather than an equal amount.

There is also a second framework that can be employed to answer the question of what constitutes equal treatment. Here the appeal is to an ideal of political and social equality. If our aim is to achieve a society in which people are treated equally, then we must take into account the amount of suffering caused by our punishment system. And fining two people who have widely disparate amounts of money the same amount does not harm one nearly as much as the other. If the amount of the fine is the same in the two cases we are not living up to the ideal of equality: we are favoring those with more money.

Either framework within which the question can be located points to the desirability of making equal treatment in the present case a matter of levying fines based on income (or wealth.)

In fact, some countries do that in such cases as traffic tickets. See http://www.sfgate.com/news/article/Speeding-fines-being-linked-to-income-in-Europe-3275939.php

There are many other kinds of case in which the need to talk about what constitutes equal treatment before the law raises its head. Those need to be considered on their own merits. But they do need to be considered. Our public discussions are not yet that advanced.

The Fetus as Person
(with Juan Matute)

Presidential candidate Bernie Sanders gave an excellent speech at

Liberty University. However, it had a significant flaw. That had to do with what he said about abortion.

The current standard liberal, leftish, defense of abortion, the one employed by Sanders, focuses on a woman's right to control her own body. However, a well-primed anti-abortion opponent knows exactly how to reply to that. There was just such a student in the audience who was quoted in the media following the talk. She asked (I don't have the exact words) "But what about the other body?" Her objection, and it is widely used by those opposed to abortion, is that there are two people involved and to mention only the rights of one of them, the woman, is to ignore the rights of the other, the fetal person. Opponents of abortion find that a very powerful reply. References to a woman's right to control what happens to her own body will not disrupt the objection in the slightest.

The only way to support abortion in the face of that quite common objection is to deny what it assumes, namely that the fetus is a person, is a human being.

That same student said, supporting the crucial assumption, "Science and philosophy have shown that the fetus is a human being."

First, consider the appeal to science. Science could not possibly show what she (and others) claim it has - for the terms 'human' and 'human being' (and 'person') are moral and legal terms not scientific terms. The scientific term for what we are biologically is 'homo sapiens'. Now the human fetus is not even a member of the species homo sapiens – it is a homo sapiens fetus. And if we do say that it is a human fetus, we do not mean that it is a human being but rather it is the fetus of something having the moral and legal status of a human being. (Here is where all the talk of its potential for becoming a homo sapiens, even a human being, comes in.)

So science could not possibly show what she claimed. As for philosophy, my guess from being a member of that tribe, is that the overwhelming majority of philosophers will deny that a human fetus is a human being (more or less on the grounds I employ above.) Suppose that even half of the philosophical community say a fetus is a human being: that does not show as she claims that philosophy has established that. Only if the overwhelming majority of philosophers were to accept that would she be right: and that is not remotely the case.

The *only* argument for the anti-abortion thesis that the human fetus is a human being is religious. (God implants a soul in the fetus at the moment of conception.) That is why the young lady appeals to science and philosophy: she, and her co-religionists, want to hide the fact that their position is solely religious.

Anyone, such as Senator Sanders, who wants to talk to the opposition (you can get away with talking of a woman's right to control her own body to an audience of progressives) about abortion has to cut to the heart of the matter and say something like 'I support abortion and disagree with you because you hold that a fetus is a person, a human being and you are mistaken about that.'

Another student asked Sanders (roughly) 'Why do you say you want to defend the most vulnerable and yet support abortion?' The assumption there is the same, namely that the fetus is a full-fledged human being, simply temporarily hidden away, unborn and is very vulnerable. It is that assumption about the personhood of the fetus that we need to reject.

A friend of mine (Juan Matute) produced an excellent version of the liberal position:
1. The pregnant woman is bearing her fetus, and she alone is giving it life.
2. The fetus is hers and hers alone, not anyone else's.
3. The pregnant woman is the one who is responsible for the nourishment and health of the fetus.
4. It is the decision of the future mother if she is able and willing to love and care for her child. If she is not, she has to make the decision whether to abort or to allow for adoption.

5. Once the fetus has left the birth canal and the body of the mother, the transition is complete and the result is a real person. Up until that point, the fetus is the "property" of the mother, and not anyone else's. 6. Once the transition from fetus to a born child is complete, the baby is a member of society and subject to all laws and regulations thereto.

The problem is that it is there assumed (see 5.) that the fetus does not become a person until birth. While that is the best view to take (I pass over the reasons for that here), it runs head on into the standard religious assumption that the fetus is a person from conception. Hence even a sophisticated defense of abortion such as this will make no impact on those who reject the practice as morally mistaken. Once again, until the crux of the issue is confronted there will be a stand off.

The Morality of Capitalism
By Bob Gerecke, Ivan Light and Merrill Ring

Does capitalism have a moral center? Three essays.

(1) What Happened to the Moral Center of American Capitalism?
By Bob Gerecke

Robert Reich recently asked the question 'What Happened to the Moral Center of American Capitalism?' Let me try to answer. Reich implies that once upon a time there was a moral center to capitalism in this country.

Was capitalism moral when the businesses were locally owned and operated by people whose customers and employees were neighbors?

In my wife's small upstate New York town of only 1,500, the merchants cheated their customers and employees. During high school she worked in a food store, where the owner stood to one side of the large round scale when weighing flour and other bulk goods, so that from his angle the needle would look like a full load when it was less. He insisted that she do the same. She refused and quit.

A few years later, when local businesses were audited by the government, the audit discovered that both she and her mother had been cheated by paying them less than the full amount of the minimum wage for the total hours worked. After this discovery, both she and her mother received checks from their former local employers.

During high school I lived in a town of 8,000 and worked briefly in a locally-owned grocery store. Day after day the owner would give me a 15-minute task 5 minutes before quitting time. I asked an older employee about this, and he said this was how the owner obtained some unpaid labor. I quit.

When health insurance was being debated, I read two reports which proved that doctors in private practice adjusted their advice to generate money for themselves. In one study, two counties in California were compared. The county with fewer patients per doctor prescribed far more visits and treatments for the same problems than the county with more patients per doctor. The treatment outcomes were the same in both counties. In the other study, two counties in Texas were compared. In one the doctors had investments in hospitals and laboratories; in the other, they didn't. Doctors prescribed far more hospital visits and lab tests in the first county than in the second, for the same problems, with equivalent outcomes.

Small capitalism wasn't and isn't necessarily ethical.

Big capitalism involves an even greater risk of unethical behavior, because the absentee investor and the CEO can demand maximum results without becoming involved in the messy details of how to get them, and the employees are trapped by fear of job loss or co-opted by rewards.

Some businesses crow that their employees are paid salary rather than commission, so they can be trusted to give the customers good advice. This itself is an admission that economic incentives generate anti-social behavior.

Capitalism isn't moral; it's neutral at best and a source of temptation at worst. It motivates anti-social as well as socially beneficial behavior. The wisecrack that "business ethics" is an oxymoron isn't far off course.

Some -- perhaps most -- people cannot resist the temptation to act unethically when it's financially advantageous. In recessions, it may even be necessary to survive. Once it's been done without penalty, a psychological line has been crossed, and it will be crossed again. Laws, regulations and their enforcement are necessary to protect us.

If we're not careful, the profit motive can even infect public service. We have read that police in some areas target minorities for minor infractions, that police are sometimes under pressure to write many tickets, and that police have used laws to seize property from people who are accused of crimes but never convicted. Can you imagine how many children would be put in foster care if social workers received commissions from the foster homes? Or how many would be left with their parents to be abused further if the workers received bonuses for avoiding foster care? Can you imagine how high court awards would be in civil cases if the judges and juries received a cut? Can you imagine how many shoddily-built buildings would be approved by the inspectors if they received bribes for doing it, as occurs in countries where public employees are poorly paid? Bribery and bonuses insert the profit motive into the public sector. The person who is paid an adequate fixed salary is liberated to do what's right and is more likely to do so, in my opinion.

The profit motive impedes ethical behavior. A system that relies on it has -- and never had -- a moral center.

(2) The Moral Defense of Capitalism at Its Inception
By Ivan Light

Bob Gerecke's question is so good that I wanted to offer in support what I know of the academic literature that deals with it. I have also had my personal brushes with cut-throat capitalism, recollecting especially the summer I sold the Crowell Collier encyclopedia door to door as a student, and was taught to lie to customers about the "special deal" they were getting.

Beyond anecdotes, there's now no dispute that markets are amoral (not immoral). Even the defenders of market capitalism acknowledge that. Their defense of capitalism turns on its efficiency in giving people what they want and allocating resources to this purpose in the economy. If people want snuff films, capitalism will provide them. If they want gasoline, capitalism will provide all they want.

That said, Bob Gerecke says that a profit-driven system *cannot* be an ethical system "and never was." Here I must disagree. That is the old-time religion, and it's really old. Aristotle condemned production and trade of commodities for exactly Bob's reason. As for the Romans, a bit later, they thought that the god Mercury was the patron of both thieves and merchants. Similarly, Hindus and Chinese classically ranked merchants below peasants in their social status hierarchy, and above only prostitutes. Moral condemnation was, we now believe, the ubiquitously hostile view of market capitalism in the traditional, pre-modern era.

Arguing against the old-time view *a century ago*, the German sociologist Max Weber went back to the origins of modern capitalism in the sixteenth century when it, then an economic innovation, expressed what Weber called "the Protestant ethic." By that term he meant that Protestantism, especially Calvinist Protestantism, conferred a moral legitimation on market capitalism that the system had never previously enjoyed. This legitimation helped early capitalism to survive the moral condemnation of the Roman Catholic church.

In a nutshell, the Calvinist legitimation of capitalism worked like this. Sure, one can relieve human suffering by giving one's money to the poor as the Catholics recommended, but that method does not eliminate poverty. It just offers transitory relief to some poor people. A million dollars will provide one dollar for a million people if given away as charity. It is far *more moral* to invest one's million dollars in a productive enterprise that creates employment and provides high-quality wholesome products to the public at a reasonable price. That way the money initially invested continues to do *good work forever* rather than being dissipated in one fell swoop by donation to the poor.

To accomplish this productive investment, the Protestant theologians recommended a life of hard work, reinvestment of profits in the business, and a personally ascetic life style. No booze, no dancing, no luxury, just hard work. Moreover, since anyone who lived that way would naturally prosper, the Calvinist theologians concluded that capitalists were doing God's work. So he blessed them. Wealth acquired in trade then became a sign of divine election and poverty a sign that the impoverished person was a no-good idler, abandoned by God in this life and condemned to hell in the next.

There's more to say, but let me point out the lingering implications of this theology even among those who don't go to any church. Being rich is meritorious. Poverty is a result of laziness. That is why Donald Trump should be the next President of the United States. That is also why the welfare state should be abolished. Indeed, if you hear someone say, "that God-damned" Joe Blow did this or that reprehensible thing, what's asserted is that God damned Joe Blow to perdition. His misconduct is only proof of that divine disfavor.

Here in America, an exceptional land, a city built on a hill, we cannot get away from our cultural heritage any more than they can in Iraq, Iran, or Saudi Arabia.

(3) Morality and Capitalism: Some Comments
By Merrill Ring

Opening apology: forgive my failure to mention all relevant failures and benefits of capitalism. And especially forgive me for talking of capitalism as if it were a single economic system.

The (partial) disagreement between Bob Gerecke and Ivan Light over whether capitalism has a "moral center" requires some commentary.

Light correctly points out that markets are amoral: firms that participate in them are not required or expected to take into account moral issues in making decisions. For instance, you fire Joe, quite a good person, because he is not needed by your company and you retain Sam because he is valuable to the company even though he is a moral failure; their differing moral qualities simply are not to be taken into consideration in your business decisions. Again, you move your plant elsewhere because you can make more money that way and are not required to think of the hardship created in the local community (neither the old nor the new) by the move.

However, the question of the "moral center" of the system remains. Gerecke and Light point to quite different matters in their disagreement. Gerecke emphasizes that, in the pursuit of profits, those in business are encouraged by the system, by the motivation built into the market system, to do the morally wrong thing. Light agrees, offering an anecdote of his own in support. And, of course, those anecdotes could be multiplied many times over. There must somewhere in the academic literature be studies of how individuals in a system built on the profit motive are put under pressure to act wrongly. (Barbara Ehrenreich's *Nickled and Dimed* is a great narrative of the how the system produces pressures on the lowest level of workers.)

Light says that at least once upon a time there was a "moral center" to capitalism and defends that by calling attention to matters quite different from how the pursuit of profits tends to cause the pursuer to act wrongly. In talking about how Protestant theologians in the early modern era defended capitalism as a morally significant economic system, Light, and the theologians, run together two different considerations in support of that view.

Capitalism was defended by Protestant theologians as a superior way of achieving the moral ends of what had been the province of charity. If you want to seriously help people, it is better to do so by engaging in productive activities than by providing them with charity. The moral center that Light refers to rests upon the idea that capitalism is a better means than the going economic organization for providing for the economic well-being of the entire community but especially of those who are poor. Capitalism is better than charity.

Light, however, also notices a different line of argument the Calvinist theologians used to defend a capitalist economic system. This second kind of defense concerns not the poor and how to provide for their needs, but rather concerns what Weber famously called 'the Protestant Ethic'. Something was needed to spur people into those productive activities which were aimed at alleviating the plight of the poor. Light nicely spells out the set of ideas that was created to justify the life of capitalist money-making. However, despite the occurrence of the word 'ethic' in its name, the Protestant Ethic is not a system of morality, a set of moral beliefs. When we encourage people to have a better work ethic we are not urging moral improvement on them. The great athletes who have a great work ethic (say Kobe Bryant or Albert Pujols) are not thereby morally great persons.

Morality has to do with our relations to others – the Protestant Ethic is more like a work ethic, encouraging individuals to behave a certain way for their own good. Of course, as the word 'Ethic' makes clear it is very easy to slide from a set of ideas about how a person should behave to the idea that living in that way, living by those precepts, is a matter of morality. Light's final words remind us of just that: that our judgments of the rich and of the poor are treated as if they were moral judgments. Having worked to make money does not make one a morally better person and not being interested in engaging in productive work does not render someone a moral failure. That Americans respond otherwise is, as Light says, a matter of our cultural history.

The War on Christianity

Are Christians being discriminated against in the U.S.? Of course not! For all I know there are pockets where some Christian or Christian institution or practice is being discriminated against — but they are so insignificant in the total story that the possibility can be duly noted and set aside.

The claim of discrimination is misguided but not without some basis in fact. What looks to be discrimination is the weakening of Christianity as the 'official' religion of the country. When a city says that a Nativity scene cannot be erected on public property, as it may have been for years, that is not discrimination. It is the realization on the part of the city that it has been allowing a practice that is expressive of a particular religion. That, the city has come to realize, is unconstitutional and so the practice is to be henceforth prohibited.

That is not discrimination against Christianity — it is a recognition of what the law in the country is and that it has been violated for some time. Nor is the existence of that law, in other words the constitution in which there is no official religion, not even that the country is officially a religious entity, a sign of discrimination against Christianity.

No other religion is being granted the right to erect a similar item expressive of its religious views, a move that might provide evidence for discrimination against Christianity.

Nor is such a prohibition giving preference to atheism or any such thing. There is no widely recognized symbol for atheism, but if there were, the prohibition, done on constitutional grounds, would cover not only religious symbols but also anti-religious symbols.

Those who complain that such prohibitions are pieces of anti-Christian discrimination have clearly failed to understand what discrimination is and have failed to understand what constitutionally this country is. And that failure is tied up with the fact that the country is slowly recognizing we are officially a secular country, leaving religion to be not a government matter but a matter of personal belief.

The loss of undeserved past privilege does not amount to

discrimination. It is the loss of past privilege that those Christians who claim current discrimination are suffering.

Rejecting the Blue Lives Matter Movement

Blue Lives Matter is a police, and police supporters', response to the Black Lives Matter movement. It is tempting to say that it is a wholly misguided response, an expression of thoughtless loyalty. Given the statistics about the police shootings of blacks, the appropriate response by those in the police would seem to be 'We are ashamed of the role of our fellow officers in the large number of killings of black citizens. We pledge to join with Black Lives Matter in reforming American policing.'

Still, that is not the entire story. For it avoids the question about the role of loyalty, solidarity, *fraternite*, in human life. Surely solidarity is something valuable, a virtue, an excellence for people. It plays an even larger part in at least some types of organization in which the people involved seriously depend upon each other – and certainly police departments are one such kind of organization. It is to be hoped and expected that members of the police will display a significant solidarity with other police.

Which of course raises the important issue: what are the limits of a person's or group's loyalty when it is known that some members of the group engage in acts that violate moral and/or legal standards? That, of course, is a long debated question with no single general answer.

What is disturbing, in the end, about the Blue Lives Matter response is that it shows that loyalty is being placed above every other consideration, above moral standards, without even any thought about the proper limits to loyalty to the group and its members. In short, Blue Lives Matter is a morally unacceptable movement.

Getting the Whole Loaf and Going for it Now

Several significant fundamental political issues are being explicitly raised in the Democratic primary campaign. (Nothing like that is happening in the Republican primary.) Those (connected) issues concern the value of experience versus judgment in an elected official, the importance of continuity versus change (or evolution v revolution) in the public life of the country, whether it is having a vision of what needs to be done or the ability to achieve results that is the crux of political leadership.

Paul Krugman has been claiming that Bernie Sanders and his supporters are on the wrong side of at least two of those issues. Sanders and friends are "idealists" and that is a very bad thing for Krugman.

Politics, according to Krugman and others, is about getting "half a loaf" instead of the idealist's effort to get "the whole loaf".

Robert Reich has the beginning of a good reply to Krugman. Krugman's view assumes that the loaf in question is at least a decent sized one. But imagine, Reich says, that the whole loaf is small. Let us think of it as only a French roll. If so, a half loaf amounts to very little, certainly not enough to sustain body and soul.

Reich's way of filling out Krugman's analogy needs to be supplemented, to be made less quantitative. What if the whole loaf is (also?) stale or even moldy? If we aim only at a half loaf, we would be, according to the picture held up by Krugman as the very essence of good politics, working to achieve half of what none of us would want.

To be less analogical, what if the range of allowable ideas in the political arena is narrow and out of date, contain nothing by way of what a vision of a better world and life would be? If we then follow Krugman's advice, aim at nothing more than a part of what is on the market, we shall be politically crippled.

Good politics starts with examining orthodox ideas about where we are and what is possible. Krugman knows that about economics – but he is so dedicated to these limited pictures of what politics is about and by a commitment to Hillary Clinton, the he cannot give sensible directions to political action. Bernie Sanders starts with a critique of our situation and the standard ideas for improving it and then fashions an account of what is needed. Both the critique and the projection of what a significantly better life would be are part of politics too.

Politics is not being a technician, about knowing how to cut the loaf, but is crucially about what kind of thing we are cutting and about having a vision of what is needed.

Obama has been notorious for thinking that he could offer a cut loaf to his Republican opponents (offer a compromise) instead of asking for it all and then seeing what they were willing/able to compromise on. So he ended up getting (at best) a quarter loaf. He has no vision about having a vision nor has Krugman. Bernie has one. If he has to compromise in the face of recalcitrant opposition so be it – but you have to start with the ideas, with the vision, with a good wholesome whole loaf.

Krugman has also been defending the idea that incrementalism, continuity with small gains, is the way to effect change. He is mistaken about that too.

I have some young friends, with two children under 6, living in Houston. They badly want to get out of Texas with its noxious moral, intellectual and political ambiance, for their own sake and for the development of the children. They want to get back to the west coast.

Suppose Krugman were to offer them advice. "Do not think of moving too far west in one swoop: that's being idealistic. You should aim at Dallas – it is westerly but not too far. Then in maybe 4 or 8 years, if the world cooperates, you can take another westward step – say to Austin. That way, in the bye and bye, you will make it all the way to your goal, to the blest coast. And along the way don't dream too often of where you want to end up – be happy that you are taking steps in the right direction. It is still Texas you will be in but, hey, you can't have everything in one move. Imagining that you can is baloney idealism."

So if you are in a bad place and can conceive of a good place, don't try to get there in one step – small increments are the way to go.

There is an important distinction that must be kept in mind here. To have as a *policy* taking only small steps is one thing, a bad one. It is like telling the alcoholic to cut back one drink at a time and to be pleased that she/he is making progress: some day you will be on the wagon. That is not the same as an intelligent piece of advice: reminding those who proposed changes that there will be opposition, that not all your goals are going to accomplished smoothly. That is not advice about how to act, that is not policy advice: it is good advice about what to expect on the way.

Krugman is not offering a reminder of the difficulties of achieving your aims – the policy of incrementalism is not an external hindrance: it erects prior limitations upon how to act.

Bernie Sanders is not an idealist: he knows perfectly well that there are huge roadblocks to pulling off what he is advocating. He knows perfectly well, and says, that he can't accomplish those aims by himself. It will require a "revolution" – that is, a massive effort on the part of the citizens of this country will be necessary to break the power of the 1%. That is not idealism (unless you are a deep pessimist and think that the power of the elite is so entrenched and overwhelming that it cannot be broken.)

On Being Great

Murray Kempton said when Lyndon Johnson announced the Great Society that he would prefer a good one.

That insight is quite relevant today when we hear that Vladimir Putin and Donald Trump – an odd couple - want to make their respective countries great again.

At least for countries, being great does not require being good – in fact, achieving greatness may well preclude being good. A friend of mine once noticed that Hitler was not just a very very naughty man. Naughtiness and evil do not exist on the same scale. So too, perhaps to our surprise, greatness and goodness are not on the same scale.

For a country to achieve greatness seems to require power, dominance, war. Both Putin's actions and Trump's words show that that is what they have in mind when they call their people to greatness.

For my part, like Kempton, I would prefer that we strive hard to be a good society. And that we choose leaders who aim elsewhere – not lower but elsewhere - than greatness.

Patriotism

I had seen Michael Moore's new documentary *What to Invade Next* and was discussing its interest and power with my son. He told me that a co-worker had said of Moore's films 'Why should I see them? They are so unpatriotic.'

I was once again astonished at such a conception of patriotism. Moore is hugely patriotic – he desperately wants his country to become a better place to live and he spends a large amount of time, energy and money trying to make us see that we both need to be better and that it can be accomplished.

Socrates said at his trial that he was a gadfly to Athens, sent by the gods to sting the huge sluggish city into paying attention – and now that they had sentenced him to death, tired of his stings, they were going to find what they had lost. One doesn't have to think that Michael Moore is the Socrates of our country to notice that his mission is that of a gadfly.

How Do Progressives Slice Up the Electorate?

Joan Walsh is a most sensible commentator. But being sensible doesn't work when you are playing in the wrong stadium.

Bernie Sanders is not trying to build a coalition of either white voters and especially not of white working class voters. Look at who are attending his rallies, who are fastening on his bumper stickers: they are not working class. But they are importantly white – but to focus upon that first is a mistake.

Walsh is operating out of (a version of) identity politics – Sanders is trying to set that model aside. If you want to characterize what he is up to it is that he is trying to structure our political discourse around the Occupy slogan, namely the distinction between the 99% and the 1%. In that, the difference between white and black, females and males, young and old, working and middle class, and so on vanish. 99% of us, no matter what those other distinctions, are in the same boat. Walsh simply cannot see that Sanders' is trying to change the game of how we slice up the sides in our political lives.

For those who see the aim and actions of Bernie's campaign that way, there remains a problem of why black voters do not see what is going on. I think that there are several non-competing explanations of that – or better that the explanation must refer to several different themes. But that is a discussion for another day.

The crucial thing is to realize that Bernie is trying to slice the pie in a different manner, a manner crucially connected to the Occupy Movement. It is unfortunate that he and his campaign are unable to articulate what they are up to in terms that would enable Walsh and others to see how he is attempting to shift our way of thinking of who we are to ally with.

Open Letter to President Obama

Mr. President: It has been reported that last week you were advising Bernie Sanders' supporters that the time has come to abandon his campaign and unite behind Hillary. Let me set aside for now the young people whom Bernie has energized and concentrate only upon those of us who have been engaged in politics for some time. Should we accept your advice, to now throw our efforts behind Hillary Clinton? The answer has to be No. To understand why we must not give up on the Sanders' campaign, it is necessary to understand both the history of our present circumstances and its logic.

Our, that is we Sanders' supporters, long term view is that the Democratic Party for some time now has been mired in a set of ideas and in a number of connections to persons and institutions from which it is necessary to escape in order to fully move this country forward. We might call those ideas and relationships The Democratic Establishment or the Wall Street-Corporations-Democratic complex. Your advice to get behind Hillary now is a recommendation that we accept the establishment view of things.

We who are now supporting Bernie thought in 2008 that in you, Mr. President, we had found someone who was free of the grip of that view. We thought that you would be a transformational President, that you would be a new version of FDR. No doubt that was a piece of self-delusion on our part. But how could a very intelligent and well-educated young black man not see the direction the country needed to go? You did challenge the status quo on Iraq and we assumed that that was a sign that you were importantly free from the blandishments of other snares of the establishment. We noticed that you did say in the campaign that you would be a unifier – no doubt it was dumb to do so but we took that as campaign rhetoric from someone who must know that the powers in the country had to be confronted not coddled?

I still clearly remember the screams of bewildered pain when your early appointment of Geithner and Summers as your economic team was announced. We were sure we had a President who would lead us out of the past and here he was immediately crawling in bed with the enemy.

That was the start of our realization that you were thoroughly enmeshed in the status quo and that we would have to wait for someone else to come along who was able to avoid being caught in that set of ideas and connections that have become Democratic orthodoxy.

And then along came Elizabeth Warren recognizing that the rules are rigged in favor of the rich and powerful. She was followed by Bernie Sanders with an even broader vision. They both have what you lack: despite your command of rhetoric you do not have the capacity to explain to the American people where we are and what must be done to move the party and the country away from the ground zero. So we progressives, after such disappointment, latched on to them with joy.

Now you, having been comfortable with the insiders all along (to our surprise), are asking us return to the security of the establishment. We, however, are not going to surrender to the forces that you accepted and that Hillary champions so well. And if the world does not work out as it should, if Hillary wins the nomination of the Democratic Party, we shall have to find some way of opposing the dark side, i.e. Trump, Cruz and the entire Republican party, without embracing what has become mainstream within the Democratic Party.

Final note: the young who have been galvanized into action by Bernie are not likely to heed a call to support Hillary. As in Shakespeare, the reply to he who claims to be able to call spirits from the vasty deep is 'But will they come when you call for them?' Those young who Bernie has energized with a new and different picture of how things might be have no historical ties to the Democratic Party and to establishment thinking: you may call them to switch allegiance but they have no special reason to do so. To get them to unite behind Hillary is going to require not advice from you, or even from Bernie, but a public recognition of the power of his message and a promise that the Democratic Party will move in that direction.

Equality and Inequality

Those of us on the left are committed to equality, to working to achieve a political order in which people are treated as equals. That is what is aimed at, for, of course, equality remains an ideal, not a description of how things are. Inequalities are rampant, some of them declining, some advancing.

Now to the main project: there are mistakes that progressives too often make in talking about equality. Some of those mistakes are what I want to address here.

First, equality is not the ultimate excellence that we are trying to achieve. The fundamental goal is justice – we on the left are trying to achieve a just society. The connection between justice and equality is that the left's vision of a just society is that it is a society of equals.

The conservative, of course, rejects that ideal: for them, the just society is hierarchical, the top of the heap going to those people with whatever particular quality the particular conservative thinks most important (birth, wealth, intelligence, gender, religion).

However, the 'leveling' instinct of the left does not mean that we believe that the equality we are seeking is applicable to every aspect of life. No one has insisted that the just society is one where everyone weighs the same (or, plug in whatever silly thing you can imagine.) The range of what we are to be equal in is considerably more restricted and likely to be somewhat different at different times.

Consider the Equal Rights Amendment ("Equality of rights under the law shall not be denied or abridged by the United States or by any State on account of sex"), a matter not on the front burner right now. It was aimed at gender equality as a matter of legal standing. It did not require, say, equal pay for equal work for men and women where inequalities were not caused by the law. But of course equal pay for equal work could be (and is) and aim of progressive policy.

So if the left holds that it stands for equality, the standard response of the right is directed toward the presumed aim of equality of income (and wealth.) The right argues that that is an aim impossible to accomplish and that therefore the left's search for equality is a pipe-dream and needs to be surrendered.

Some of those claims are right, some very wrong. Perhaps once upon a time, a standard left idea was that a just society requires equality of income/wealth. I don't know whether that is true or not, but it is possible. However, the left has long since given up on that. No one today argues that we are seeking a political order in which everyone has the same amount of money. The left has come to recognize that that is an impossible aim and so no longer accepts it as the requirement for a just society.

It does not follow, as the right alleges, that therefore the left must give up on the interpretation of justice as equality. Rather what it shows is that the left is attentive to the ways of the world and is willing to surrender a particular idea when the facts run against it. However, realizing that equality will not work in this particular respect does not require abandoning attempts to achieve equality in other relevant matters. Just as the possibility of justified lies does not impugn the importance of the principle that lying is wrong, so too equalities that cannot be achieved do not impugn equality as an aim.

What the progressive can, of course, do is to try to lessen inequalities as much as can be achieved. In the case at hand, there is no strictly determined amount or percentage that constitutes the minimum inequality of wealth/income acceptable in a just society. Where that limit is will always be a matter of examination and experiment.

But today we are nowhere near that limit. Financial inequality has grown massively over recent decades (and we were never at a likely limit in the first place.) The left can, is and will work to institute a greater equality in that arena of our lives.

There are those on the left who say that we ought to stop talking about equality and settle instead for talk of reducing inequalities. That is quite mistaken. For opposition to inequalities is unintelligible apart from the idea that equality is the guiding principle. And there is absolutely nothing illegitimate about retaining equality as the ideal while recognizing that sometimes equality will not be achieved and that we must settle for a minimum inequality.

Taking a Knee

Once again those who prefer form to substance are making a scene.

Conservatives have been flipping out since Colin Kaepernick of the San Francisco 49ers started kneeling rather than standing for the national anthem in protest over the large number of shootings of, especially, black males. Kaepernick's protest has spread in football circles and even beyond: star soccer player Megan Rapinoe of the Seattle Reign and the U.S. Women's National team has joined in.

I am reminded of the Vietnam days and the protests over flag burning and draft card burning and other means of protesting – which raised the hackles of those who ran around saying 'My country right or wrong'. Of course, those who protest, then and now, know perfectly well that it is their country and are protesting precisely because it is their country. They are not protesting at the playing of, say, the Russian or Moldovan national anthem. It is because they are American that they are protesting at the American anthem.

Moreover, I am impressed by how respectful the kneeling protest is. The form of protest could be giving the finger, mooning during the anthem, and who knows what else might be thought of. In fact, kneeling might have been the convention adopted by the country to express respect for the country. While the right worries about form, they are unwilling to face the issues being raised by the protesters.

Political Correctness

The notion of political correctness is a big favorite of the right-wing. The basic idea is that of people saying something political because it is the socially expected thing to say.

Those on the right who think our political discourse is rife with political correctness have a point. They first notice that their own inclination to belittle those of another race or gender or sexual orientation or ethnic background or religion or … is not approved of in current polite public discourse. So to get along, they stifle their impulses. And they then wisely guess that there are lots of others who are doing that too.

Along comes someone who accepts their impulses and then approves of their speaking their mind, their prejudices. So we get a flurry of charges of political correctness about their own previous silence or verbal acceptance of what they did not believe in their heart of hearts. And then the charge is that the others who really believe as they do but speak otherwise are still engaged in political correctness.

But there are two different kinds of case. On the one hand, the idea that everyone who, say, condemns anti-Muslim sentiments must be engaged in political correctness, that they must either be a (secret) Muslim or else engaged in political correctness is wildly mistaken. Some people, and it is to be hoped lots of people do, contrary to right-wing assumptions, genuinely believe that it is wrong to belittle those who hold (say) religious beliefs different from their own. Now the crucial questions: are those who have come to believe that pure of heart? If not, are they not engaged in political correctness?

The answer is No to both questions. What the right-wing refuses to recognize is that there is such a thing as moral realization and that even when one has a change of heart in a matter of morality that does not mean that every contrary impulse is immediately wiped from one's psyche. That none of us are pure of heart is a fact of human life. Genuine moral understanding is perfectly compatible with the past still tugging at us now and then, producing thoughts and feelings incompatible with our new grasp of how things are.

For such people, to refuse to publically articulate those prejudices of the past is not political correctness. For that is a term of criticism. And it is praiseworthy that people refuse to help maintain their old moral views by giving in to the impulses and speaking them. (It is of course a different question about how people must confront the lingering prejudices to themselves – that is not the issue here however.)

Are We Political or Economic Animals?

One of the, perhaps the, chief objection to the TPP, is the provision that a frustrated economic actor, a corporation usually, may sue, in a private and restricted court, a foreign government whose policies have caused its frustration by eliminating or restricting some economic activity the actor had planned for within the borders of the particular government. (Note: that has been a feature of many other so-called 'trade agreements' not just the TPP.) That is the ISDS provision (investor-State Dispute Settlement).

The provision is the outcome of the work of law professor Richard A. Epstein, a hero of the libertarian movement (and, mistakenly, of the Tea Party.) In fact, Epstein's work justifies similar actions within a country: if the government of the U.S. accepts a policy that limits the expected profits of an American economic actor, on Epstein's view that actor should be entitled to sue the U.S. government for loss. In either its broad or narrow application, Epstein's idea is based on the assumption that our human economic activity is more basic than our human political activity – interference from the political sphere with economic activity involves an illegitimate reach of the humanly less basic aspect of our lives into something at the root of who we are, namely our economic lives.

A more full discussion of these matters waits for another time. What can be noted now is that the progressive vision flips the Epstein view upside down: as Aristotle said we are political animals. Our economic activity is nested within our political and social lives, supported by them, made possible by them.

Conceptions of America

Agreeing with Bannon!!

Before Trump became an official candidate, in one of his appearances on Steve Bannon's show on Breitbart (so I hear), he said something about an economic issue and Bannon replied (so I hear): "A country is more than an economy; we're a civic society." (Of course he meant the generalization 'a country is a civic society.')

To my astonishment I agree with Bannon on that matter.

That is to say, when doing political analysis one must talk about more than the state of the economy. And Bannon's implicit claim, that in that mix of considerations those "civic" matters sometimes outweigh purely economic issues, seems to me quite correct also.

Tom Frank's *What's the Matter with Kansas* notes that Kansans consistently vote against their own economic interests – and regards that as lunacy. For Frank there is no other intelligible motive than the economic.

I have many friends who regard our invasion of Iraq as drive by nothing more than the desire to acquire Iraq's oil. While that is a motive that the Bush administration tried to hide, nonetheless the will to power was itself an important part of the reason why we invaded. There is evidence that those who voted for Trump were not the real down and outers of our current economy. Rather they were people who were getting by but who had significant non-economic resentments and motives. Had they not had those resentments and motives, had they acted solely on economic grounds, they might have joined the Democratic Party and voted for Bernie Sanders.

The identity politics of the Democratic Party is based on much else than economic considerations. Bernie had a rough time in many places because he wanted to shift the party, and the country, to a class politics and did not know how to build into his argument recognition that there is more to our political life than the economy.

So, Bannon is right: whether the political analysis is of why some particular thing is done or whether it is a matter of what we ought to do, there are considerations to be taken into account other than the economic interests of the actors.

Disagreeing with Bannon.

Bannon contrasts the economy with what he calls "civic society" – 'civil society' would have been better. Where he and I part company is over how we are to conceive of our civil society.

One of the consequences of our recent election has been the emergence onto the national stage of a certain conception of what America is all about, one that denies what has been the central conception of recent times.

The conception that has become prominent in connection with the election is named by its proponents the alt-right position. It presents itself under that title as an alternative conservative view, alternative to the standard conservativism of American politics. In what respects it is an alternative to orthodox conservativism will be discussed below.

While talking of that view, progressives should not accept the title assigned it by its supporters. It is best to name it what it is: it is best labeled white suprematist (white nationalism, white nativism). That name needs expansion but that should wait until the contrasting conception is sketched out.

What we progressives have been trying to achieve – of course we haven't come anywhere near full success yet – is what I would call an *equality* conception of America. Others would perhaps prefer to label it multi-culturalism. I think the view that has become mainstream with the recent election simply speaks of it as liberalism.

Before going further in setting out the views, there is one thing that must be noted. Both those competing conceptions in the first instance do not explicitly involve economic matters. In the end economic considerations must be added in, but the aim of both on the face of it have to do with cultural matters (or in Bannon's term civic society) where those matters are contrasted with economic considerations.

It is widely recognized that the American right, so-called American conservativism, divides into two. There is the economic wing. That position has been in the conservative saddle. The self-named alt-right sees itself as representing the other wing, the branch that has not been in the saddle. Its central concern is with cultural issues. It is that form of conservativism that has emerged as a consequence of 2016 into the limelight. Those who belong to it think (rightly) that while they have provided the votes for conservatism, the economic wing has managed to run the show. At last, the alternative position has emerged from the shadows.

The triumphant white suprematist movement includes not only the idea that whites should rule but along with that central racial theme a commitment to a basic European superiority, male dominance, heterosexuality, Christianity, anti-intellectualism, and other positions.

Those ideas are what Bannon conceives of as constituting American civil society, what we should be like.

By contrast, the equality, or multi-cultural, conception of America denies that we are a white nation in the sense that we are a country in which whites are *rightfully privileged* because they are white. Rather we are (to be) a country in which people of different races (in so far as the notion of 'race' has any theoretical import) live together as equals. So too in this conception, the United States is not by nature, though it is by history, a European country – different ethnicities are welcome here and add enormously to our lives as Americans. An aim is to make men and women equal partners – to accept that people have different sexual inclinations – to hold that no religion is privileged, that different religions, and atheism too, are as American as apple pie – that the ability to use our rational capacities should be prized – and so on.

That equality conception has been slowly becoming the central conception of American life. And that fact is an important part of why the white suprematist conception has muscled its way onto the main stage in consequence of the 2016 election. For those seeing this country in that way have been losing their hold on power, both political power and conceptual dominance. In significant part, the electoral victory of Donald Trump is a consequence of the losers staging a counter-attack, having found a spokesman for their realization that they and their views are no longer the epi-center of American life.

Those differing conceptions of who we should be and the realization on the part of both groups that the flow of power has been toward the equality conception are deep elements in our psyches, part of our conception of our country and consequently of ourselves as individual people.

The post-election anti-Trump demonstrations are by those who have seen the equality conception of who we are temporarily (it is hoped) overcome by the electoral counter-attack. The white suprematists, those who embody Bannon's view of "civic society", are starting to realize that while the Presidential election has gone their way, their opponents are not going to go quietly – and so they too are taking to the streets in defense of privilege and inequality: not so much economic privilege and economic inequality, but of the particular culture in which our economic system has historically been embedded.

Where are the Conservatives Today?

There They Go Again! It would be a giant stretch to call the healthcare bill considered by the House a *conservative* measure. Conservatives are supposed to conserve: at their best they accept improvements to the community after having carefully considered its (financial) cost and thinking through its impact on maintaining the community.

The proposed health care bill – which involves the repeal of the ACA and constitutes its replacement – can by no stretch of the imagination constitute a maintenance of the community or a furthering of the well-being of the community: its non-financial costs are far too high to be that. The supporters of the bill are radicals masquerading as conservatives. It is time for the American media to name them correctly.

The Conservative Governor of California: When asked about The Healthy California Act (SB 562), a bill that proposes that California have its own single payer health care system, Governor Jerry Brown's answer was "Where do you get the extra money? This is the whole question."

Now that is the answer of a *genuine* conservative: the "whole question" has to do with money, with how one pays for a proposed project. There is no question at all about whether it is a good proposal or a needed project. There is no point to discussing issues about the excellence of the proposal until the money question is settled.

That is what a true conservative is: someone who asks of a progressive policy how it is to be paid for.

Asking that question is the function of conservatives in a political system.

So-called conservatives get themselves and the country into serious trouble when they start having ideas themselves. There are very few real conservatives left running around out there. But Jerry Brown is one.

(Well, sometimes he does have non-monetary thoughts, ideas – but we all have our failures.)

Extremism

I was reminded the other day of the 1964 slogan written by Harry Jaffa for Barry Goldwater's 1964 presidential campaign: "Extremism in the defense of liberty is no vice".

That is as bad today as it was then. In fact, I can imagine it being used by ISIS in its recruitment material. Do we really think that anything goes in the pursuit of freedom? Or maybe anything way out toward the end of the scale?

Suppose we don't imagine the situation being that of seeking liberty from a foreign power (say the colonies rebelling against England) but that of freedom within a settled nation, say within the United States at present. Should we all be applauding Cliven Bundy and friends who are certainly seeking freedom (from regulations about public lands)? What are we willing to allow them to do? Blow up the local headquarters of the Bureau of Land Management? Is that not extremism in the defense of liberty?

To say that extremism in the pursuit of anything very valuable is "no vice" is to say that it is a virtue, something to be commended. But surely the entire talk of extremism and what the Jaffa/Goldwater slogan is criticizing, namely moderation in the pursuit of liberty, is not how we need to be thinking of the situation at all. The real aim should be to be thinking of particular acts and of whether they are justified or not. Does my pursuit of my freedom justify me in taking your property or your life? Should I be free to shoot you because you are taking a shower in a house I own (an actual case)? Those are the questions that need to be asked, the terminology that needs to be used, rather than that of extremism and moderation.

Notice that the conservative view expressed by Goldwater and Jaffa is so typically American: freedom is the highest value and outweighs everything else. We do not have the slogan 'Extremism in the defense of justice is no vice'. That freedom is the ultimate value is why matters of justice have such a difficult time getting traction in this country – pursuit of justice is always to be outweighed by considerations of freedom.